D0102731

great americans

great americans

famous names, real people

written and photographed by kk ottesen

BLOOMSBURY

Copyright © 2003 by KK Ottesen

All rights reserved. No part of this book may be used or reproduced in any manner
whatsoever without written permission from the Publisher except in the case of brief
quotations embodied in critical articles or reviews. For information address Bloomsbury,
175 Fifth Avenue, New York, N.Y. 10010

Published by Bloomsbury, New York and London
Distributed to the trade by Holtzbrinck Publishers

Library of Congress Cataloging-in-Publication Data has been applied for

ISBN 1-58234-296-2

First U.S. Edition 2003

10 9 8 7 6 5 4 3 2 1

Design by Elizabeth Van Itallie
Printed and bound by C & C Offset Printing Co., Ltd., Hong Kong

for my family

contents

introduction

As your car speeds below a lighted window among a thousand just like it in the Bronx, or past one lone home nestled in the hills of rural West Virginia, do you ever peer out and wonder: *What would it be like to live here? What do people here think about? What do they do? What are their stories?*

Within the sprawling boundaries of this vast and varied country, our lives are shaped by an extraordinary range of factors—location, age, family, gender, race, religion, occupation, culture, wealth, health, humor, ideology, ethnicity, education, experience, and certainly fate. Sure, we call ourselves Americans, but how is my life in a fourteen-by-fourteen-square-foot New York apartment similar to yours on thousands of open acres in Montana? What is it that we share? What *does* it mean to be an American?

Driven by the desire to understand what people of such different circumstances could possibly have in common, I searched for a way to experience a truly random cross section of life across the country. At last it came to me: Why not use the very names that have shaped the country to examine what it has become today? Traveling to each state, I would find and interview someone who shares the name of a famous—or infamous—American icon. And I would ask these people about their daily lives, about what they think it means to be an American.

With the idea burning in the back of my mind, I'd stay late at work, casting about for a way to put the idea into motion. Things began to take shape when I stumbled onto several online search engines that had compiled the white pages from all over the country. I'll never forget the thrill when I first typed "Marilyn Monroe" and, seconds later, forty-one Marilyn Monroe addresses and phone numbers stared back as nonchalantly as if they'd been Marilyn MacQueens, Smiths, or Joneses. Who knew?

After contacting folks and arranging interviews, I zigzagged around and across the country in my '98 Chevy to meet these contemporary "great Americans" on their home turf—a casino in Vegas, a sorority house in Ohio, a shrimp boat in South Carolina, an east Tennessee dairy farm, a wings joint in Houston, a correctional facility in northern Vermont, the Big-O Tire Shop in Globe, Arizona, and living rooms and kitchens in urban, rural, and suburban neighborhoods from inner-city D.C. to coastal Alaska.

In each new city, at each address, it was impossible to predict who would open the door. And that is the beauty of the project. While initially I thought I would interview a few people from each state and with each name, it became clear that there was no need to overengineer the project. Every person I met had a fascinating, complex world to share. From all walks of life, and every state in the union, the "great Americans" whose words and images make up this volume speak individually and in aggregate to the diversity and commonality of American life.

Although many of the people I interviewed were perplexed by my undertaking, all were surprisingly supportive. They offered sodas, meals, directions, and accommodations in their homes, no matter how grand or humble their circumstances. They spoke of failures, disappointments, and dreams. They shared advice on love and marriage and opinions on everything from politics to salvation. Whether sales clerk, cancer scientist, politician, or rancher yuppie, hillbilly, soccer dad, or separatist, all generously gave me the privilege of a glimpse into their homes, their minds, and their hearts. And offered, for a few moments, the opportunity to take a walk in their shoes.

Their thoughtful and earnest responses continue to impress and humble me. And knowing them continues to be a privilege beyond even my initial hopes. What emerges from my journey—really their journeys, and indeed all of ours—is a candid testament to the courage and dignity of the American experiment. A mosaic of people. A composite of the country in this moment. And one we could glimpse only in talking to strangers—albeit those we know by name.

—KK Ottesen

great americans

I've done all kinds of hard labor all of my life.
And I still ain't afraid of it.

john adams

Swanton, Vermont
72 years old

I corresponded with the superintendent and then John Adams's caseworker, who set up our meeting one morning at the Swanton Correctional Facility, just miles from the Canadian border. We sat in a small room off his unit's main activities room and talked for quite some time about his many experiences, daily life as an inmate, and the twists of fate that lead you there.

Mr. Adams told me that he'd been working on making friends not associated with the bar life he'd had for so many years and had recently met some nice folks while mowing lawns. He had been looking forward to moving down to Florida, as he'd recently decided to do, but seemed comfortable waiting things out. He was most concerned about a cat he'd been taking care of, though he knew the landlord of the property his camper's on would be looking after him.

I was named after my father. You see, my father and mother come from Lithuania. He landed in Ellis Island and then he sent over after the girl he was courtin' and they got married over in this country. And when he got his citizenship papers, he could turn his name—which meant John Adams in Lithuanian—to the American name.

I took a lot of pride in my work. I've been a carpenter all my life. I used to build—I didn't build a whole A&P—but I used to build the cupola that went on top of the roof there, used to always have a wind pane on it. I used to be so proud I'd take the children and my wife for a ride, then I'd drive by the A&P and I say, "You see that cupola up there? I built that." "You see that house there? I built that." I was proud of stuff like that.

I have a daughter in St. Petersburg, Florida. And I had a son in Tampa but he died of Agent Orange. Married, three times . . . all of them wound up in a divorce. I don't have any family in Vermont. But I like the people of Vermont.

I been incarcerated four months. All told. Been here roughly around seven, eight weeks. Yeah, they just moved you different places where they had room. 'Course, never been tried yet or sentenced or nothin' yet. DUI and driving while my license suspended. I don't know how much time I'm gonna get. Last time I had to serve around three years.

Oh, it's not bad . . . When I was in Rutland they had them three men to a cell and the man sleeping on the floor, see. Two men per cell here, yeah, that's it. Yup. There's no men on the floor here.

It is the same old thing every day. I play solitary because it's hard to get anybody in here even to play cards . . . There's all different types

of people here. I am probably the oldest one. They allow you to come out of your room at six o'clock in the mornin'. And then they allow you to go outside. I walk around the track. You can wear your regular clothes here all the while. Now in the D unit, they take your clothes away from you and give you like a jumpsuit . . .

You're not in here because you're perfect, I mean there is some sort of behavior and they are trying to straighten you out before they turn you loose. I take Social Skills and I have to go to Substance Abuse, because that takes in drinking . . . I mean, I never get violent when I'm drinking, but my biggest part is I'm not afraid to get behind the wheel of a car without a driver's license.

I take it seriously. I've learned a lot about drinking. I've learned that it's been the ruination of me as far as ever making anything out of myself. When my marriage broke up and my family broke up, I drank pretty heavy then. But I ain't been drunk right down-and-out in I betcha fifteen or twenty years, I mean like when you go home and fall upstairs instead of falling downstairs . . . I was working on it to change it—in fact, I was paying fifty dollars a week to go to an alcohol counselor, and I was gonna sell all my stuff and move down to Florida with my daughter. I'd let up a lot on my drinking.

I never did nothing much for my children. And that's why I wanted to move to Florida, because my daughter owns some property down there and she wants to build an A-frame. I'm not too old to work and I'd like to go down there and give her what she wants, build an A-frame for her. That's about my biggest dream.

Well, I'd rather be out than be in here, I wouldn't say I'm proud to be in here, but . . . make the best of it, that's all I can do. What else can you do? ∎

What does it mean to be an American? Oh God, I don't know. I mean, what is America? I question this here now. When I was younger, in '45, when my brother and them went to war, I mean they didn't have to draft 'em; they was glad to go to war. But today, I'm glad the young kids running away from war, because young guys' lives are going over these politicians getting rich. I'm glad I'm my age and I'm glad my children is all raised up, because I wouldn't want to be bringing up no children today.

No regrets. That's probably what I live by. You only live once. Go and see and do what you can while you can.

samuel patrick adams

Pierre, South Dakota
18 years old
50 years old

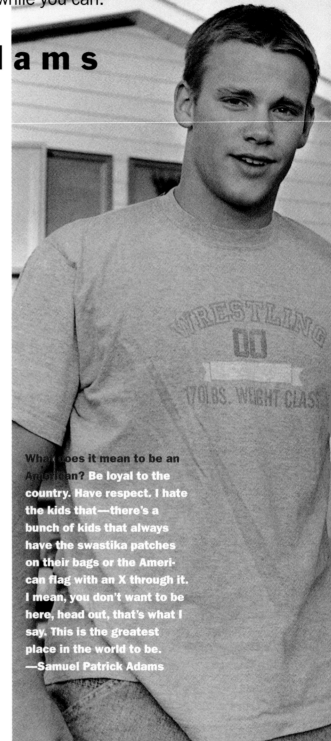

What does it mean to be an American? Be loyal to the country. Have respect. I hate the kids that—there's a bunch of kids that always have the swastika patches on their bags or the American flag with an X through it. I mean, you don't want to be here, head out, that's what I say. This is the greatest place in the world to be.
—Samuel Patrick Adams

I interviewed Sam Adams—the father—on my summer 2000 trip cross-country. As I was taking his picture outside their home on the outskirts of Pierre, his son, Samuel Patrick Adams, aka Pat, came home from work. I particularly liked this shot of the two of them. Since I was driving through South Dakota on my way from Nebraska to North Dakota nearly two years later, and since they share the famous name, I liked the idea of interviewing the younger Samuel Adams as well, for a father-son spread. And it was nice to check in again.

Despite the fact that his grandmother and mother were right at hand and sometimes chimed in, Pat seemed totally unselfconscious. Said his mother: "He's as near perfect a son as you could wish for." With the easy self-deprecation of the adored, Pat commented: "She's a little biased. Probably."

Both father and son remarked that their name enjoys far greater renown as beer than as founding father these days. And for the record, Sam Adams prefers Budweiser.

Been here forever. Right here. Pierre, South Dakota. I love it. Same house. I'm in high school. Let's see, right now I have a 3.65. My goal is to graduate with a 3.5 and never study or do homework. Senioritis.

College'll be different. One of my good friends, he's playing football with me. We're going to room together. We've all been together for our whole life, since we were little tykes. They always joke, call me All-American Pat. Another one of my buddies is gonna play basketball up there. So, there's three of us. I'm ready to go. It's time for something new, you know. Being on your own—but not really on your own yet.

Me and one of my friends, we're going to take a semester off, or after graduation, and we're going to head to Europe. Pick up odd jobs, bartenders, I don't know. Just travel, you know, find a girl with an accent. We've talked about it forever—I think we're going to do it. I don't know, France, Spain, Germany, just wherever.

My biggest dream . . . Anything in the world? Be an actor. Famous. Have a lot of money. I've thought about being a teacher, coach, I don't know. I'm up in the air. Salesman, teacher, like a P.E. teacher—is there ever a day in their life they're not happy? You play games with kids. Another dream job, being like a head guy for a big corporation.

I want to get out of South Dakota for a while. Ten years, maybe. I want to live in New York City. You got to live in New York City, it's the Rome of today. But I want to come back. I want to raise kids here. Right here in Pierre, I think. I'd rather have a family here.

I want to be able to say in forty years: I have no regrets, I've done what I wanted, you know, not have a midlife crisis and "Oh, I wanted to do this and I never did . . ." You know? ∎

What does it mean to be an American? Freedom! I'm glad to be an American. And I like my part of America. Right here. And I like to be able to go to other parts of America. You can kind of feel at home. Except for New York City maybe . . . I don't know if I'll ever make it there.
—Sam Adams

I'm proud of my family, my place, my country.

sam adams

I'll come down here sometimes in the wintertime, in the middle of the night, when it's blowin' and cold, and look out the back window, and it just looks like it could kill ya. It's life threatening. How those homesteaders survived in the winter is beyond me. I tell you what, they were tough.

See, I'm Samuel Pierce Adams, Jr., so he's Samuel Patrick. I didn't want to make him a third—too hoity-toity. I was born in Sioux Falls and my dad's family is from there. My mother's family is Scandinavian, first-generation immigrant, from a little, little place in northeastern South Dakota, right in the Indian reservation.

I've lived in San Francisco and Los Angeles for a while. A lot different from here. This, this is my kind of life. Especially here, right on the Missouri River. It's real nice and there's no people. A hundred miles in any direction to find any other town that's comparable in size. Otherwise, just little hamlets.

I work for UPS, so I drive out all these back roads—about 250 to 300 miles every day. I have an extended area. Go to all the ranches and all the places like that. I only have a few years before I'm going to retire.

Then I hunt and fish and play golf and that's about it. I got bit by the golf bug for the last three, four years. I wish I would have golfed when I was younger, but I didn't. I'm kind of a political person.

Dreams? I just want to be comfortable and live happy . . . right here. I'm not going to go anywhere. When I retire, I want to stay right here. I've often thought about doing nature photography instead of hunting. I look forward to it. Even though I don't want to whisk my life away. The winters and all that kind of stuff are nice. That'd be very nice if you didn't have to get up and go to work in it. If it was real bad you could just stay in. ∎

Walk every day with a smile on your face, and love everyone. You have no idea what magic it does. People smile right back—it's contagious.

muhammad ali

Minneapolis, Minnesota
19 years old

I met up with Muhammad Ali at a hopping coffee shop, a favorite of his, on the University of Minnesota campus. Ironically, I'd found a link to his website while searching online for his more famous counterpart's address—to avoid accidentally sending the icon himself a letter.

During our conversation, Ali moved comfortably between discussions of dorm life, his neural networking research, various cultural differences (which you sensed he'd had to explain many times in basic detail), and sociopolitical issues.

He was not only thoughtful and articulate, but also earnest and optimistic, with all the freshness of an eager young thinker.

Muhammad Ali, the boxer, he's a great man, he stands for peace. He's very famous, but I will never steal his fame, because he rightfully gained it and that's my job now. To gain my own fame. So for that reason, when I introduce myself I say I'm Muhammad Abdul Ali.

But everyone calls me Ali. A-L-I. Simple. If you remember *Will and Grace* on TV, it's like: *JustJack!* I say: *JustAli!* Scares 'em to death! I say uh-LEE, but here in the Midwest they say, AAAAH-lee. I say muh-HUM-med and here they say, mo-HAM-HEAD. *Haaaaaam*. Head. Muhammad is "messenger of Allah." And Ali is basically "the devout." My full name, Mughal Chowdhary Muhammad Abdul Ali, doesn't fit on the Immigration and Naturalization form. See, naming and also lineage has a lot of importance in my culture, because we can trace our ancestry for, like, hundreds of years into the past. If you apply Arabian traditions, my name will turn out to be, like, *thiiiiiiis* big, because it's bin Abdul Khaliq bin Abdul Ghani, meaning son of Khaliq, son of Ghani, and it keeps on going. I love my name.

You notice that when I'm speaking I'll say "Yahh," and stuff like that. But see, I'm proud of the accent that I have. I'm glad that I grew up in Minnesota. Newscasters and broadcasters always come to the Midwest to get the training because that's where the language is just, like, understandable to everyone. Minnesota, I personally think, is *the* best place to live—except the weather's pretty bad. Minnesota is the second most progressive state in the entire union. For godsakes, we have a wrestler as a governor!

I was born in Pakistan. One of the reasons that we had to leave was that, although I'm a Muslim, I'm an Ahmadi Muslim. And Ahmadis are ones that actually take a very scientific approach to the Koran. We will not just listen to some statement in the Koran and take that for verbatim. We're actually going to analyze that. For that reason, we're persecuted.

Contrary to what happened in New York—Muslims, by nature—as Christians, by nature—are *pacifists*. The day that happened, September eleventh, my parents immediately called me up and they told me to stay indoors, because I do look from the Middle East. When I was walking back from a class, three guys started yelling at me, calling me "terrorist." Fortunately, a couple of my friends recognized that I was in trouble, and when those guys started heading towards me, took care of the situation. People were dumb enough that they asked me, "So now, how do you rationalize your support for this?" And I was like, "I, I don't support it at all . . . "

If you go back far enough you'll realize that my ancestors were actually Jews, because Jews and Muslims are brother and sister. But they hate each other, because they have different versions of the same story. I like to overlook that. Instead of all this history and everything, I just say, why don't we just believe in something called love. That's how I operate.

Family is something that I'm very proud of. We're really, really tight. I mean when one of my friends would call me up in high school, they'd be like, "Do you want to go the mall or something?" I'd be like, "I want to hang out with my family today." Dinner for us is like one of the most fun times, because we eat for the first hour. After that, we have our tea at about like ten o'clock, and then we usually end up talking until about like three in the morning. That's how super-close of a family we are.

What does it mean to be an American? That we have the world's best and safest home. One thing that annoys me to death is children–slash–college students that say: _America is one of the world's worst places to live._ Yes, America does have some things that are bad, but you know what? America is a _million_ times better than any other country out there. What we have, other people cry out for. A place to call home, a place to be safe, a place which tolerates you, a place that lets creativity and diversity flourish. In Pakistan, my family had to live every single day of their lives with the fear that something might come and hurt us. In America, our security is guaranteed. Fairness—judicially, legally— is guaranteed. Security is what it all comes down to. And then tolerance. I say America is the best place to live—but I won't say God bless America . . . because I believe there's a separation.

Basically, when we came here, we said, we're going to stick with our cultural traditions and everything. That's important to us. Take for example my sisters. Pakistani girls are supposed to dress in a modest way—not for the reason of men telling them, but for the reason that they see their body as a jewel only to be presented to one man, the husband. My sisters do accordingly, but in a new, cosmopolitan style.

In comparison to my family, my sisters and I are a bit more liberal. When it comes to like social issues such as gays, lesbians, stuff like that, abortion, I'm pretty much a bleeding-heart liberal. And I make my rationale scientifically. If you put yourself in the place of the Israelites, well, they were a small tribe and they wanted to become larger, so it would only make sense you want to procreate. That's my take on it.

My studies are very important to me. Throughout my high school career, I did research in neuroscience. I created a hybrid neural networking algorithm. And for that, I got fourth place at the International Science and Engineering Fair, and a lot of scholarship money. It pays for most of my tuition here at the University of Minnesota.

My classes are just awesome. Right now I'm taking Chemistry Two, Calc One, History of Early America, Political Science, and Biology. If there was a test tomorrow, then I'd probably study until about four. I must do my best. And if I lose a point or two, it just really gets to me. Next semester I have _every_thing science—that's my element. Professor of Neuroscience is what I want to be when I grow up. Dr. Ali, Ph.D. . . . heh heh heh.

One-thirty is when I am done with all my classes—that's how I engineered my schedule— one-thirty to about four o'clock I go to my

work—I'm part of the computer staff. And then from four until about seven o'clock I allocate to my social life. I just have fun. Fun for me is shopping, I'm really into shopping. I love clothes, antique books. I love to go to museums, I love to go downtown.

Aside from that, I like to hang out with my friends. This campus has about 50,000 students. Quite literally, I do meet someone new every day. My friends usually are just like a hodgepodge of everything, people from all over. Diversity is something that I completely love. And I'm proud of the way that I can unite people. My friends always describe me with one word—and that's my favorite word of all time—ineffable.

After seven o'clock, I usually am going back to my studies. I get very little sleep.

I worry a _lot_. There are so many things that are happening that people just overlook. Like if you ask anyone from the United States, they will not know Ariel Sharon, policy-wise, has killed so many people that he beats Slobodan Milosevic when it comes to war crimes. I see it as intolerable. And that's why, to a degree, I detest religion—because it separates us more than unites us. I just wish everyone would get along with each other.

I want everything to be paved smoothly into the future. I just wish that I am successful in all that I do. I wish that my academics go well and I wish my family stays intact for the upcoming future. People usually get scared of the future when they _don't_ know what's going to happen. My future is so planned, I know what's going to happen, but I'm still scared of it. I don't know why. I can't put it in words.

I don't want to grow up. I mean, I so love my life as it is. ■

What does it mean to be an American? There is no place I'd rather live. We're so lucky. I'm very patriotic. Actually I give flags out 4th of July, Flag Day. This year I gave them out after 9/11. This country really needs to get to the basics. We all need to start taking our kids to church so they develop attitudes about wrong and right and integrity. If you're going to do something, do it right, those kind of things.

My grandmother use to say, "If you can't say something nice, don't say anything at all." I try to do that.

clara barton

Joppa, Maryland
54 years old

We arranged the meeting around the times Clara would be babysitting for the grandson she adores. I was warmly greeted by Max, her dog, who's a big scruffy ball of love. We sat drinking coffee and talking particularly about lessons learned in relationships, and community, and resolutions such as exercise, going out, and of course, our loyal pets.

We then went out back on her deck, which overlooks the water. Trying to get Max to participate in the photos was a riot; Clara would coax him with treats as I tried to keep his attention long enough to fire.

My standard answer with the older people who recognize the name is, "Yeah, I look damn good for my age, don't I?"—they remember it from history if they're over thirty-five, forty. This'll probably be the only way I'll be put in history! I don't think I'll ever do anything really as worthwhile and lasting as she has.

I'm a Realtor. I enjoy real estate. There's no limitations to what you can do. It's just you. Last two years I have been a top producer—well, one guy inched me out, but he had a partner, so I still claim it for last year. I'm the only one in my office that doesn't have some other means of support—a husband or a retirement pension. Yeah, you work a little harder when you have to . . . But real estate never is a nine-to-five type thing. My job is mostly on the weekends.

My biggest worry is always paying my bills. I'd love to hit the lottery. I really would! Then I could do everything that I've ever wanted to. I wouldn't tell anyone if I did. I probably would still want to do real estate but it would be for me. I'll probably keep doing real estate even when I retire—to the ocean, Ocean City.

My second husband, Barton, lived here in Joppatown. I fell in love with it. It's quiet. It's safe. I had this opportunity to buy this place. My daughter and her husband live not too far, so it's easy for them to drop the baby off. We have this beautiful grandson. He's six months and he's happy all the time.

Okay, am I happy? For the most part, yes. I'm more of a positive person than negative. I have lots of friends, a lot of single friends my age and in the evening we get together, but not every night. I enjoy being around other people. I'm independent, self-reliant. That kind of thing.

I had my father with me, and once he died I was just terribly, terribly depressed. And I went and got Max and he's what pulled me out of it, you know. With a dog I had to get up and I had to go do something, you know. I had to get out and walk him. Yeah, I love him to death, I swear. And no matter what, he loves you. And he just doesn't understand that you didn't come to see *him*. Well, you definitely have to get him in the picture too.

It would be nice to have somebody. I see some of my friends who've been married for twenty-five, thirty, forty years. Especially one I'm totally jealous of. He takes her out for lunch. They stop at a jewelry store. "Pick one out. Which one do you want?" He thinks she is just the most wonderful thing, but he thought she was just the most wonderful thing thirty or forty years ago! I want that.

But I've never had that. I've always had abusive people in one way or another. I've chosen badly I guess. But I think that women typically, they want someone so bad that they just settle. You know. The thing to do was to get married, so you latched on to somebody and it was supposed to be *forever*. That's what I did and I'm not going to do it again. The young girls today, I think, are a little more self-assured—I hope, anyway—than we were. I'm proud my daughter was self-supportive for a long time before she got married.

There would have been a time when I would have just put up with it, just to have somebody to go out with occasionally, and not anymore. Rather sit home! They're gonna have to be somebody pretty special that thinks that I'm pretty special and treats me that way. But if it doesn't happen, I'm okay. So if it happens, it happens, and if it doesn't, it won't matter. Really. ■

Just do the best you can in life, you know what I mean? Try the best you can. Just be real. Be yourself. Treat people the way you want to be treated. Give everybody the respect that you demand.

al capone

Franklinville, New Jersey
32 years old

I was lucky enough to catch Al Capone on a Saturday, his one day off. He and his father-in-law were watching the football game while his wife, Lisa, their son, Al Jr., and their young daughter were preparing to head out for the afternoon. As I listened to him talk, I was impressed by his thoughtful and unselfconscious responses to my questions. His philosophical outlook, delivered in so unpretentious a manner, struck me as quintessentially American. As he put it, "I'm the kind of person that tells you the truth no matter whether you get mad or you get glad."

Oddly enough, one of his best friends growing up in South Philly was a kid named Johnny Dillinger.

I'm into waste management. Nah, I'm only kidding! You ever watch *The Sopranos?*

Everything I do is manual labor; everything is done by these hands. I work down at a food distribution center right in South Philly. We distribute to all the Super Gs, the Acmes, Pathmarks, ShopRites. It's mostly warehouse work, that's what it is. You know, anything to do with unloading and loading the trucks, distributing and stuff like that—basic stuff. Nothing much. Nothing *exciting!*

I've been working down there for about twelve years. Six days a week. Monday to Friday, and then I work Sunday. Sunday is all right though. I don't work a full day and I get paid double time—that's a sweet check instead of a regular check. I'm trying to put my wife through college, you know, and the baby's still young. Maybe a few years and she'll start school and my wife will be out of college, and then we can make a decent living.

I always told myself that I wanted my kids to have everything that I didn't have—without spoiling them. When we were growing up, we never had a dishwasher, a microwave, never had a washer and dryer *in the house.* So when the time came when I had a pool in the backyard, a pool table, cable, and you know, VCRs everywhere and a microwave . . . You know, I was wearing the same sneakers for two, three years, you know, putting cardboard in them and stuff, while my kids are getting like three, four pairs of sneakers a year—they're not even worn out and I'm getting them a new pair!

My son's eight, and my daughter's two and a half—she'll be three in November. I'm proud of my kids, I'm proud that . . . I don't know, silly things, like being a coach for my son's team, and then we won the tournament. I had a hand in making them the champs, it's little stuff like that. Like when I see my son play ball and I see how good he is and how he can make a play, you know, can make a throw from his knees, seeing stuff like that makes me feel good. When I'm out there with twelve kids, teaching them baseball, I have so much patience. They'll come crying off the field and I'll say, "That's okay, no big deal," instead of saying, "Stop crying, boys don't cry." I don't believe in that. I think all kids cry, and I think they cry for a reason. I've always wanted to be—since I was a kid—a psychiatrist, a child psychiatrist. Because when kids have problems, you know they're not faking it. They either have the problems or they don't have the problems. They're either spoilt, or they have a problem.

My parents were very disciplined. Six children in a bad neighborhood, we grew up in a mixed neighborhood and it was always a bad neighborhood, but none of us never went to prison, never got in trouble, never picked up by the cops. I just want to be that kind of leaning as my father, but also a little more loving than my father. My father was never a bad guy, but not much on the hugging and kissing thing. But that's the older generation . . . They showed it in other different ways. But I like to be able to kiss my kids goodnight, tell them I love them, stuff like that.

Al Capone is my grandfather's first cousin—so like my third, distant cousin or something. He met him a couple times, like he came to hide out when they were searching for him. Everybody always thought he was a bad guy, but when it was the Depression, he fed like 75 to 80 percent of Chicago with the soup lines, he fed people, because nobody else could feed them because there was no welfare back then.

My mom, she said she had to name *one* of us Al, and I was the last, I was the baby, so she was running out of time. The only time it came in handy was when I got in high school and girls liked it. Otherwise, during grade school and when I was a kid it was always, you know, people ridiculing me for it: "Who do you think you are," you know, "Al Capone?!?" But I like it, I mean, people remember you. Ten years later you might see me and you'll remember my name because it's Al Capone.

I always loved God; I always loved Jesus Christ; I always believed in the Commandments and everything else, but . . . I had a lot of bad things in my life with the Catholic church. Growing up, all's the church ever wanted from us was money. So how can you get money from a poor family? You can always see that it hurt you in a way. Like recently we had a problem. We were trying to bless my son—we were both Catholic and we always went to church and stuff like that—but they wanted nothing to do with it. They didn't want to baptize him because we weren't married and we got in a whole fight with the priest and everything. So, I think it was a Lutheran church that we went around to. They didn't care that we weren't married; they just cared that there was a child that had to be blessed and they blessed the baby.

I believe that if you have religion, it should not matter with money or how you live your life, that as long as you believe and you take care of your family, there should not be a problem in the world. You shouldn't have to go every *Sun*day. I work on Sundays. They just deny you a lot. It's like a hard-headed father. You tell him it's black, he says it's white.

Politics? I'm interested at a point . . . I've always liked the Democrats because they were always for the small people. Why, with the Republicans, it's almost like a trophy. Like with Bush, he's a tycoon. He has rigs of oil, he has tons of money, he has a baseball team, now all of a sudden he wants to become President of the United States.

The only one I believed that did a good job as a president would have to be Bill Clinton. I really believe that the eight years that he was in there, or whatever it was, that he's run the country better than any other president that *I've* ever noticed. Why, with all the Republicans, like Reagan and Bush and stuff like that, we always had a problem. Prices are up on *this*, prices are up on *that*, not enough *jobs*, stuff like that. I noticed that when he got in there, everything seemed to straighten out and everybody seemed to have a job and there wasn't so much violence. It just seemed like it was a lot easier with him. Why a lot of people criticize him because his extramarital things . . . As long as he runs the country all right, I don't care if he's a drag queen.

I guess the minute I wake up in the morning and my kids wake up and my family's healthy, and there's nothing wrong, I'm happy. You know I have my times, everybody gets depressed, unhappy at times. I guess you can never be completely happy with your life, you know? I mean if everybody wanted to be totally happy in their life, everybody would have a ton of money, have exactly the house they want, you know the kids and the wife *per*-fect, but life is not perfect, you know? But for what's happened in my life, I'm happy, you know? Like I said, I got a roof over my head, I got two cars. I got two kids. We're all healthy. We eat, we're alive, and I have a lot more than I had when I was a kid, so I'm, I'm happy. ∎

What does it mean to be an American? Oh, it's a big thing to be an American. It's huge. You get to vote, you get to live your life the way you want. You can be a lazy person, an energetic mover, a go-getter, anything. It's the only place that you can come and you're poor and you can end up one of the richest. I mean, you can say what you want to say—people in other countries are put to death for that stuff. Or beaten. I think it's the single best thing in my life to be an American. It's unlimited.

> I really don't worry about anything, you know. I think that makes you old. I *hope* that everything's gonna be all right. And I think it will.

charlie chaplin

Seabrook, South Carolina
64 years old

Charlie was a lot of fun. We met downtown and then caravanned back to his boat, where his wife, Ann, joined us. He teased and joked and got more outrageous through the meeting, at one point striking Sports Illustrated Swimsuit Issue–style poses in imitation of the 7UP TV commercial where a group of paunched drivers do the same. (Only later did I see the commercial and howl with laughter.)

He generously offered to let me "camp" on his boat for the evening, an invitation I gratefully accepted. So when he, Ann, and their amazing palm-sized dog, Midget, headed back home, I watched the sun set and enjoyed a peaceful evening without cell phone or email coverage. When I went up to my car to get my toothbrush, I met a neighbor and friend of the Chaplins. He invited me to join his family for a beer and nachos . . . another wonderful surprise. I learned from his daughter, Ziggy, an area real estate agent, that Forrest Gump had been filmed downtown in magical, Spanish moss–draped historic Beaufort (BYEW-fahd).

My mama told me, "We didn't name you after Charlie Chaplin the comedian. But, it's good. Look at, he's a famous man!" Every time you said, "Well, my name is Charlie Chaplin," "Oh yeah?! You that funny man?" Well, I am . . . not just him. Always say, "Not the rich and famous." He was run out of the country because he was considered a communist. I don't think he was either. I just think that was something that was going on then.

I was born in Port Royal and I know everybody. No—I know everybody that's my age. Port Royal is one of the oldest towns in the United States. It was founded in seventeen-somethin'. It's grown, Hilton Head's right there, and they have aaaaaall the big people coming out.

I'm a commercial fisherman. Shrimp. When I'm working, I go out at four o'clock in the morning and I quit at nine o'clock at night. We drag the nets, we put 'em overboard, we pick 'em up and clean 'em up. I run the boat so the guy that's working with me, he's back there cleaning up shrimp while I'm going where we supposed to go. I pull out my net average every fifteen minutes, go back and look in it . . . and if it's gotten ten shrimp, put it back out, and the next time if I got thirty shrimp, I'll turn around and go back and do that same track. I mean *exactly* that same line. Got it figured down to the shrimp ain't got a chance!

A fella leases a dock from the state in Fort Royal and he buys all the shrimp from everybody. And he put 'em on a truck and sends 'em to where you live, New York. They say that's fresh shrimp, but it *can't* be, you know they've probably froze them three times . . . *We* sell 'em to him for three dollars a pound, he sells 'em to somebody else, and he trucks 'em up there and y'all pay about eleven dollars a pound. Ho ho heh. Or more. But we see on TV in New York, you pay like a thousand dollars a month for an apartment! I can't imagine . . .

You know, it's hard to make a living. The last few years we've been restricted to using things in our nets to stop catching turtles and fish. And it's cut us down. Most of the shrimp now comes from somewhere else. Like China and other countries. See, they don't have them restrictions like we got, so shrimp from there is cheaper. And we have a thing in South Carolina, they call it "recreational fishing." They throw bait out and it draw the shrimp and they're allowed to catch forty-eight quarts . . . a *night*. That hurts everybody.

When the season's bad enough I work during the winter at different jobs to get by. And it's been bad, yeah it has. Construction, you know, like dock building and building bridges. But my wife works, and I'm old enough to draw social security, so, you know, we getting by. But sometimes it ain't easy. And I had prostate cancer, too. Wheew! I'm a veteran so I can go to the VA Hospital. They said it's gone.

I pray and I believe in God. But I don't go to church. I got a lot of friends, like this friend, he's a biker and he's real religious, and he thinks I'm not religious or something because I drink. I drink beer and I drink brandy. And I smoke like a fiend. My wife, both of us are Methodists.

Been married forty-one years. When I seen her, I said, Oh, she look good! I was twenty-two then and she was sixteen. I was sleeping on the front porch at Mama's house and she come up there with her friends. And I asked her for a date. And not too long, we was married. And I'm happy. She might not be, but I am! I'm proud of my three kids, they ain't kids, they grown up people. I think we done good. ■

What does it mean to be an American? You're free. That's the main thing. I mean you got to watch out for tax man and the policeman's gonna get you for doing something wrong. You can do what you want to do. And in other countries you can't. You know you might go to jail and stay there forever and they won't even look back at you. But if you're in the United States, even if you go to jail, at least they'll come back and say later on, "Well, whatchyou doing back there?" You know, "We forgot you" or something. You're always looked out for. And people don't realize it till they go to the other countries. It's respect for each other. It is a big difference.

What does it mean to be an American? I always say "North American," 'cause that's my Dad's hangup . . . I think it means freedom to choose how you want to live your life. That's what I'd like it to mean. I mean, we have the choice on paper, but I don't think we authentically live that way. There's a lot of pressure to be something that you're not. I think we take for granted the right to protest and to disagree and to be the lone voice . . . that's part of being American.

Be okay with who you are. Be authentic and be genuine. Have the courage to be independent and have your own style and flair.

cesar chavez

Berkeley, California
36 years old

I met Cesar at his office at the Fox television station one evening after work, and we did the interview comfortably settled in armchairs on the set of the morning news. I'd been in Sonoma the previous day for the very moving wedding of two dear friends, and at one point in our conversation Cesar and I set each other off crying, both moved to tears by "those moments" in life where things are truly beautiful. In one of the more hilarious moments of my trip, Cesar reached for the tissue box they kept on the set presumably for just this reason.

The following morning, I took BART to his home in Berkeley, where I had the good fortune of arriving as David was making brunch. After taking some pictures as they puttered around the garden, we walked to Berkeley's farmer's market, and I took this shot as they shopped for the week and for David's upcoming trip to Burning Man. (Cesar's on the right.)

I was born in Augusta, Georgia, to two Peruvian doctors, a neurosurgeon and a pediatric neurologist. I'm the youngest of four. We're pretty tight. Spent my entire growing up in Spartanburg, South Carolina—it's weird to go back. It's like, *Oh my god, this is bizarre, people are so southern . . .*

My dad said he just liked the name. No one in South Carolina really knew who he was . . . I got a lot of questions in high school like, What *are* you? In California it means a lot more. Every day I've been here I've gotten comments.

Kids? I think we're both ready, but we haven't done the logistical planning, like who's gonna stay home and how are we gonna do it? I think David wants to take off for the first year and then I would do the same. And we hope to have someone to live in, like a nanny who speaks Spanish, 'cause I want to make sure that they continue the language. We have the paperwork. We keep pulling it out and looking at it.

I worry about down the road how I will handle my kids' questions and teasing and all that stuff. Those little grocery-store conversations, like when the stranger comes up to you and says, *I don't get it, you're two men, I don't understand . . .* It's kind of exhausting, like you never finish coming out . . . there's always someone to tell!

I was a late bloomer. I *knew*, but I was like, okay, let's close that side of the brain off . . . And I think the longer you take, the more difficult it is. Once you do it, it's kind of like, God, why didn't I do that before? But for a long time I'd compartmentalized my life. It's so much healthier and nicer and less *work* to just *be*.

Average day? David brings me a cup of coffee with cream and sugar in bed. It's wonderful. Perfect. I get up, watch the news, log on, try to catch up with a little bit of work, read the paper, and then go in to work. And I'm off and run-

ning. Everything from working with an editor and producing a spot to improving someone's script. Working with designers, picking music, looking at research to figure out what people want and how to present it in thirty seconds. Basically, packaging the news so that you will watch our newscast versus somebody else's.

As a gay Latino, I'm very sensitive to what the producers put on the air. Like, well, do you notice anything about this program? . . . There are no *people of color*! There are no gay people. Like why is the Valentine's story always hetero couples who have been married for twenty years? Hey, we're living in the Bay Area!

I try to be out by five-thirty, get home, log on—I'm a little addicted to the Internet—and then wait for David to come home, and sometimes we'll go to the gym together. Usually we'll lie on the sofa. We try to have dinner together and then before we know it, it's ten o'clock, and I watch the news and he falls asleep on the sofa. It's the good life.

We had a commitment ceremony about a year ago. Outside, in a botanical garden, with our families. It's one of those moments that I never imagined *I* would get to do. I never imagined my parents being—the gay thing was a little hard for them—so the fact that they participated . . . We did a typical Jewish wedding, 'cause he's Jewish, and they had a blessing, and it's like, *I can't believe my parents are standing in front of us and saying this to us.* I mean I was worried when I came out . . . I'm gonna start crying now . . . Because I couldn't imagine my parents ever accepting me and then they were there, and it was like: *This is amazing . . .* That was one of those moments in life.

My biggest dream at this moment would be to have enough courage to do whatever I want and the first thing out of my mouth not being, "Oh, I can't . . . " ∎

Remember that there's other ways of looking at *every*thing—and it's not just somebody else's point of view. Is the glass half empty? Is the glass half full? Or is it twice as big as it needs to be?

chris columbus

Nashua, New Hampshire
32 years old

Chris and Holly live in a pretty, green development in "the rural part of Nashua." Their seemingly model young professional life offers a few surprises, though. One is the life-size knight in full armor you pass on the landing between the first and second floors—a reminder of Chris's longstanding interest in D&D and the legends of King Arthur's court.

The second and third surprises are two giant rabbits, Benny and Suzy, each more than three feet long, roaming the immaculate white carpeting and shooting across the living room when least expected. These huge, furry creatures were clearly personalities in the household, complete with the idiosyncrasies of any pet—or housemate, for that matter. While they were fairly shy in my presence, I'm told their repertoire of tricks includes flips.

It was a funny scene and a good evening.

I say, "I'm Chris Columbus," and it usually takes a minute to sink in . . . I say, "It's okay, you can laugh." But, you know, it was good when I was growing up. Things like I ran track, and you'd go to run the 440 and lo and behold you'd be getting the good lane assignments, because people would recognize your name. And usually it was the guys that did well that got the good lanes.

My father's middle name, my grandfather's first name, and my great grandfather's first name was Salvi. My mother *wouldn't* let them do that to me. But apparently it was okay to call me Chris . . . I think they both thought it was novel and kind of fun. They both have a good sense of humor in their own way.

I'm a manufacturing engineer—mainly stainless steel tubing. Our specialty is working with the very small sizes, some diameters as small as four human hairs across. So it's kind of a niche market. I do a lot of research, looking for different things that we can do to improve the business, improve our productivity. I troubleshoot. It's a family business, great company to work for. Jack, our president, always says good morning to everybody. A real Yankee kind of thing.

I've lived in New Hampshire most of my life. People that are born in here wouldn't say that I'm a native, but I would. I'm conservative, but I was raised—and proudly raised—by a feminist to be pretty independent. I very much respect a person's right to make their own choices, and that goes for just about everything. The baseline rule being: pursue your happiness but don't do it at the expense of others. I don't agree with extremist groups like the Aryans or Black Panthers who have so much rage that they're blind to the fact that there's another person behind what they're putting down.

I've always enjoyed things like the Arthurian legends, Robin Hood. And now I get online and play EverQuest with some people I know. It's the three-dimensional type of interface with multiple players and several chat channels for different usage. Let's think here . . . at peak times, you know, Saturday afternoon, there are like 2,200 people on each server and they've got twenty to thirty servers. I don't know if I'm *good*, I'd say I try to be knowledgeable. The more you know, the more prepared you are. There are so many different types of, like, magical swords, character classes, spells, books of magical items . . . I enjoy being this encyclopedia of useless knowledge. As far as getting into that kind of gaming, I have played Dungeons and Dragons—you know, the engineer, Dungeons and Dragons geek—with a group of friends probably since late junior high, since about 1986.

I'm fortunate and proud that I've got several really good friends. I can't even put a number . . . less than ten and more than five people that I know that I can count on. That I could call anytime in an emergency, day or night, and they'd be there. And I'd like to think that I would do the same. And these are people outside my family.

I'm happy that I have found somebody—I waited a long time and actually Holly waited a long time too: this is our first marriage. But that I found somebody that is so good to be with. And that we're both happy. We've been married about ten months now.

As a young professional person, I think there are, you know, milestones . . . Right now, I think Holly and I want to move into a house. So, making sure that we have enough money to put a decent down payment on it and also looking into retirement. But I don't worry about finances day to day or month to month; I live pretty comfortably. While everybody can't always do everything they always thought they would do, I have a pretty happy life, I'm pretty fortunate. ∎

20

What does it mean to be an American? A lot of it's tied to the concept of freedom. It's a country where someone can start out in a very underprivileged setting and bring themselves to a very comfortable way of life. It goes both ways too. It's a country where somebody that can grow up very, very, very privileged can completely obliterate themselves without trying too hard.

I still have the dream of having a college education and having a big house and a fast car.

davey crockett

Old Town, Maine
30 years old

I might have scheduled the Maine interview during the summertime . . . but, probably more appropriately, I donned my layers and traveled north to meet Davey Crockett on a snowy January day. I was catching him before he headed into work for the evening, and we sat around the cozy kitchen table drinking coffee and comparing stories. A native Mainer from the Portland area, Davey is the youngest of seven. He told me all about winter antics on Sebago Lake—like cookies in the snow ("when you spin your rear wheels in a circle so you keep going around and around. And make, like, a blizzard all around"). When he noticed that we both drive the same make and model, he naturally asked, "Have you gone top speed in your Prizm? My car does a buck twenty."

I also enjoyed meeting Natalia, his wife, who returned home with their young daughter and joined the conversation.

Davey Crockett actually met his wife in the woods in the University of Maine. I was walking down the bike path and that's where I met her. She was in the middle of the woods, as in Russia, looking for mushrooms.

Natalia's from a desert country—right next to Afghanistan. Turkmenistan. She came over on the Muskee Fellowship Program. Basically, the United States was paying for her schooling and she signed an agreement that when she was done with her schooling, she had to go back home. Right now, we're fighting immigration so that she can stay. We don't know what way that's gonna go . . .

2000 was a rough year. I bought the brand-new car and the debts were piling up. I was working two jobs and my wife was working two jobs and we're just scraping by. Then they took away her work authorization and I stopped working one of my jobs and started going back to school. And then I got the job at General Electric, a CNC machinist, and stopped going to school.

So, with a lot of overtime now, I'm trying to pay down debts. General Electric's got a rule you can only work twelve hours straight in one day, so that's what I try to do. I work three-thirty at night to midnight. Pick up shifts from other people that are giving 'em up. Just get the most work in so I can to pay off the bills. Every, every day. It just depends on if there's a shift, you know, and a machine open that I know to operate. So a lot has to do with luck, what other people are working, and what machines are on the list. It takes a while to actually learn how to get in there as much as you can!

And I'm proud of, well, I'm a Persian Gulf war veteran. I'm a Bronze Star for my actions while I was there, and also made sergeant. I'm proud of my wife and my daughter, too. I'm proud to be a machinist at General Electric. And I'm proud I have a commercial driver's license.

I went to school for tractor-trailer truck driving. After working from ten o'clock at night 'til seven o'clock in the morning I would go straight to school from work on Saturdays and Sundays and stand around outside in the cold. And drive these tractor-trailer trucks around the yard, like doing back-in maneuvers and taking turns. We started in the coldest part of the year. And ended in the snowiest part of the year. I used to wear like two hoods over my head from like three jackets, and I would wear three pairs of pants and two pairs of socks and insulated boots, and I actually stood out there just stuffed with clothing. I'd sit behind the wheel of a truck and my stomach would be touching the steering wheel. From all the clothes I had on.

The day that they gave the test there was like a huge blizzard. You have to actually parallel park a tractor-trailer truck. And you have to back a tractor-trailer truck up so that when it parks with its trailer up against the loading dock it has to be in "jack," which is almost a ninety-degree angle. I was the only one that passed in my group that day. My brother drives a truck. So he was happy and proud that his brother got in on it, too.

In General Electric my wages went up and I had enough of a debt to income ratio to get a loan to consolidate some of my credit cards from the bank. So I squared myself away . . . that's something to be proud of, at thirty years old. Eventually we will be there. ∎

What does it mean to be an American? Well, it seems like we all struggle with debt. You know, I look at other countries and how they look at us. It feels like we have a lot, you know, but we also have a lot of work to do to have the things that we have. And we're constantly under a pressure of global competition. Here in Maine, shoe factories have closed down. The Mainers made the molds and then they moved the factories overseas. Because once a mold's made, they do the shoes for cheap, with cheap labor.

What does it mean to be an American? What I *like* about it is just my freedoms. I definitely have a problem with the ACLU in certain respects as far as getting too much rope to hang yourself. But I'm thankful that I live here and very proud of the United States. We take for granted more things in the United States than most people have a right to even think about. I believe everybody in the world shares something in common, we're all from the same seed, basically. It's just our egos and our foolishness that separates us.

> I tell my boys, be careful how you treat people . . . you're gonna get it back. If at all possible, give a sucker an even break. You know, first time out, trust everybody until proven you can't.

james dean

Bismarck, North Dakota
48 years old

After we talked at the Deans' kitchen table—James Dean is full of stories, explanations, facts—he showed me some of the mineral samples he'd collected while gold prospecting. He gave me a garage-based gold panning lesson and showed me a number of the more interesting pieces he'd collected at area sites. Then he drove us over to his current prospecting area, with a quick tour on the way of the historic (abandoned) Indian mound village that neighbors it. It was a gorgeous, clear, windy day: bright white tufts on an expansive blue sky. Dean was equipped with a metal detector, but he warned me that we might not be able to get down to the river's edge for prospecting because it had rained recently. I figured he took me for some city slicker and was ready to prove him wrong. The incline was awfully steep, though, and did indeed look like a mudslide waiting to happen.

So I settled for a view and explanation from up high. I loved his enthusiasm for prospecting and the evident curiosity about so much of what surrounded him. And I was impressed by his honesty, his satisfaction, and his commitment to his sons.

I married a girl, she was from up here. She got homesick so we came back here. I shoulda never came back. What the hell am I gonna do in North Dakota, you know? I've been selling cars since 1991 till March. I can do it and I can make money at it, but it's not my favorite thing to do. I'm looking for something else.

You have to make good money to have kids. North Dakota, good money is three to four thousand dollars a month. Terrible, terrible paying jobs in North Dakota.

I have managed to get fired from every job I've ever had. I got fired at one job three times. Yeah. Just every once in a while I'd say the wrong thing to the wrong person. But it's kind of a mutual thing. It's just time to go. Having my own business—that's by far the best thing I've done. And I've done it twice now.

Ended up getting divorced. She remarried. When I married her, I was her boss, and she married her boss again, I'll take the kids and the house, you can go have fun. Stay here probably until my kids get old enough. I got lots of boys: nineteen, seventeen, fourteen, and twelve. The twelve-year-old'll be thirteen here pretty soon, so at least for another four or five years I'll be here. After that, who knows?

After I got divorced, 'course these two oldest kind of took advantage of the situation. I came home one night, it was sixty some people in here. Cops were here. Some girl O.D.'d on cough medicine. They said, "Did you know this was going on?" I said, "*No.* What is going on?" "Well, here's your son, I'll let him explain it to you."

My oldest son, the guy that opened the door for you, is James Dean. I'm a James Dean, and my dad was a James Dean. He just died in February at ninety-one years old.

Religion kept me going. Through the divorce, through my things with work. I have a very, very deep faith and very strong belief in God, in Jesus Christ. Years ago I turned everything over to God and said, You're going to have to see me through whatever it may be. I always pulled myself up. It hasn't been by anything I've done or just by sheer will alone. So, I believe in miracles.

I'm a member of the GPA, by the way. Gold Prospectors of America. They give you this book here, it tells you how to go get it, okay? So this GPA owns claims so I can go anywhere in the United States, long as I'm a member, show 'em my card, get in, pan for gold, and whatever I find, I keep.

South Dakota's loaded, Montana's loaded, I'm trying to find if there's any gold up here in North Dakota. They say—because we get our water from the river—there's two and a half cents in every glass of water we drink.

There are two ways of doing it. Test-panning. You just take some dirt, throw it in your pan, and pan it out, see if there's anything in it. The other way is like right behind you, use metal detectors. And then you go along and basically get a signal, you dig it up, and see what the hell it is. I got all kinds of trinkets and stuff I can show you: piece of flint, used as a hide-scraper . . . a hammer head . . . that's fossilized wood—ancient!—back when there were still trees in North Dakota . . . *this* . . . this is not a rock, it's a meteorite. Probably my biggest dream, is just to stumble across a big chunk of gold. Just so I wouldn't have to work, so I could stay here and take care of the kids more.

Yes, as a matter of fact I'm very happy right now. I don't know how to say it. I was happy before I was married, I was happy when I was married, and I'm happy now. ∎

As long as you can be true to yourself, you'll be happy.

emily dickinson

Wilmington, Ohio
19 years old

I was looking for a way to find some younger folks to interview, so I scrolled through online ICQ white pages and found one Emily Dickinson who seemed legit. So I wrote her, and to my delight, she was real. When we finally spoke by phone, she was also refreshingly enthusiastic about participating.

When I visited her sorority house one late spring afternoon, sisters came through and chatted briefly while we talked in the front room. When I asked her what her biggest dream was, she caught me off guard with her matter-of-fact reply: "I've always wanted to be on The Real World." We went out front to take pictures, and walked around campus.

Actually, my parents did name me after the poet. I think it was just . . . kind of convenient. I might be distantly related. John Dickinson, the guy that signed the Constitution, I'm directly related to his brother.

I'll be twenty in twelve days. I'm like, *Oh my gosh, I'm not going to have a "-teen" anymore.* I'm a sophomore, a chemistry major. I'm trying to pass organic chemistry right now—it's like the hardest chem class. My classes here are so small. It's not like I'm making a pitch for the college but . . . I'm serious, like my major classes are fifteen, twenty people max. Wilmington College, it's a Quaker school. More than half commute. So we don't have a real bumping college life, but you know, you find stuff to do.

I never ever thought of me in a sorority. And then I got into sorority life, Alpha Phi Kappa, and I love it. I pretty much came into it knowing nobody. And I was really surprised at how well I mesh with everybody. I mean, I do have friends outside the sorority, but like my *best* friends are here.

My boyfriend's in our brother fraternity. We pledged at the same time. We've been dating for probably about a year and a half now—we just kind of clicked.

Actually I grew up right across campus. Big move! I've always loved this area. In fact, I think after I graduate and get a job, I want to kind of move back to this general area. Because I think—this is going to sound so cliché—but I think it's a great place to raise your kids.

My mom's my biggest hero. She's such a strong woman. She is like the do-it-all mom, you know? She can go to work for thirteen hours a day, and come home, and still be in a good mood and take care of my grandma and get everything done. She made my prom dress my senior year in high school, because I wanted a silver strapless dress and I could not find one for the life of me . . . She makes the best chicken soup, big and chunky with just a little bit of broth. I just admire her. And I admire the way she ages. I hope I age like that.

I work with my mom two or three times a week at Bill Murray Ford. It's a dealership in town. And my dad and I probably see each other about once a week. We're both just so busy. My parents are divorced. I have a brother three and a half years younger than me.

My worries . . . ? I worry about everything. I worry about, you know, if I'm going to be qualified to go to heaven when the time should come. If I'm going to pass calculus and organic, my two major classes right now. I'm worried that there's going to be a war soon. I know my boyfriend won't have to go, because it's against his religion to fight. He's a Mennonite—not plain, he's like a liberal Mennonite. I'm not sure about my cousins and my brother.

I'm really proud of the fact that I'm physically in shape and that I know I'll live healthily. I don't know many people who can go out and run fourteen miles. And, I probably have to say, I'm pretty proud of the way I've lived so far. I don't really have that many regrets. Our pledge line started out with nineteen pledges and we crossed six. So I was so proud to be one of those six. That's probably one of my proudest moments.

Even though I'm busy and sometimes I just want to pull my hair out, you know, I am really happy with what I'm doing. I don't think I would do anything different. When I came to school, I didn't really have my parents there all the time to push me. So to actually do something on my own, it's just like, *Yeah, I am a person!* ∎

What does it mean to be an American? Even though I think most Americans at some point in their life have probably taken their freedom for granted, by griping about, you know, the road construction, or you know, what have you . . . I think sometimes you just have to take a step back and realize what we have.

Be kind to all.

frederick douglass

Manassas, Virginia
58 years old

I appreciate talking to somebody. I love it! I love it. I'm trying to say, I appreciate company. You enjoy yourself. Relax and talk to me. Yeah, I appreciate it. On my average day, I don't talk to nobody.

I just stay home and drink.

I was born in Middleburg, Virginia. I grew up as a po' boy. I had six brothers and seven sisters. In that mix, I was in the middle somewhere. I had one brother younger than me. Yeah, we were all born in Middleburg, Virginia. And I was raised normal, I guess you can call it.

I used to be a laborer, a roofer and a construction worker, I guess. I used to be everything. I'm useful as I want to be. I'm not retired. I'm just out of work.

I'm not an old man. But I *think* that I'm an old man. Because I'm ill, ten years at least. But I want to be useful . . . I just do part-time work. I'm in pain myself. I do some work though. Six days a week. Two hours a day. Five-thirty in the morning. I started three or four months ago.

I like to bowl, but I can't bowl anymore. What's that thing here, on the grass . . . bocce. Okay. I love doing that. I love doing a whole lot of things that I can't do anymore. I like badminton. I love sports. I love checkers. Let me ask you a question? Do you love playing cards? Do you like playing whist or spades?

I met Joe Louis; he had big hands. I was about eight or nine. He grabbed my little old hands. I was in Middleburg . . . he came to the community center . . . shook my hand . . . grabbed my little old hand . . . I couldn't even say hello. Tears come up just thinking about it. He was a great boxer. Joe Louis. I wish somebody would've taken a picture at that time.

Excuse my tears. When I talk about Joe Louis I get tears in my eyes.

I'm a Methodist. I'm Methodist and Baptist. I couldn't live without religion. It's always been that way. I think you gotta have it to survive. I don't know. I know some people say that you're a fool if you have religion. But I have my religion and I can survive. I'm sorry if people go the wrong way, but . . .

I got a third. Frederick Douglass, Jr., and I have a third. I don't know why, but I love it. I love my name. No. Didn't nobody know anything about Douglass, Frederick Douglass. No, I don't even know how I became Frederick Douglass. When my son came along, I wanted him to be a Frederick Douglass too. My son named his son Frederick Douglass after me. He's in Texas. I get to see them at least once a year. My wife goes down there. I can't travel. I'm afraid of flying. I have four children. In Lynchburg, two in Leesburg, and one in Texas.

My son takes care of me. He loves me. I got to go to my grandson's wedding in June. My son is going to come get me. My son calls me all the time. He works in the Salvation Army. I can call him whenever I wanna call him.

I think I'm proud of being a father to my son. I really think I am being a father to my son. What would you say is the proudest thing a man could be? I'm proud to be a father to my boys. I don't want them to be like me. I want them to be better than me. You understand? I'm proud of my daughters for being dependent to themselves. Oh Lord. God, them kids. You have to be sorry sometimes because you have to let the kids go. It hurts my heart.

My biggest dream is to make their dreams come true, not mine. My days are over. I mean, you could say. I can say their happiness is my wish.

My life? I had what I made of it. ∎

I met Frederick Douglass at his apartment in northern Virginia. He was, and perhaps remains, a bit perplexed at the idea of the book. "What are you, anyway, if you don't mind if I ask? I'm not the type of person to be interviewed to the public." He was welcoming and hospitable, though, and genuinely happy to talk.

Describing his life and experiences, he'd often get sad, but he seemed resilient in returning to the moment.

With our April birthdays around the corner, he laughed and called us both April fools.

What does it mean to be an American? It's freedom to speak my own thoughts. Let me say it this way: you're a white woman, I'm a black man, okay, that's freedom. There's a Chinese man over there, if I wanna talk to him, I can talk to him. That's freedom. Lord have mercy. I got somebody to understand me. It's not the way it is, but the way I would like it to be.

What does it mean to be an American? I love America. You probably hear the same thing all the time. I know the people that wrote the Constitution were all white, male, land-owning, slave-owning merchants who were in it for the money, you know, but the Constitution— I think it's the most glorious document ever written.

McDonald's and slavery and you know, cops beating the crap out of somebody, that's real ugly and stuff. I don't like that. But I just think it's the greatest idea. You don't even have to call it "American," just the idea, the concept: whoever you are, whatever you are, you have a chance to make it.

I think America is the hope of the world.

Sometimes they ask me if I'm related. I say, "In spirit."

b o b   d y l a n

Las Vegas, Nevada
46 years old

After a furious dash across the desert from L.A., in a car so packed with boxes I literally could barely move, I met Bob at the Hard Rock Cafe on the Strip. It was too noisy for tape-recording, so we relocated across the street to the Subway sandwich shop. He was casual, wry, mellow, and quizzical, often turning my questions back at me. Despite my numerous attempts to wheedle certain information out of him—such as his previous name or the name of the casino in which he worked—he pleasantly but resolutely side-stepped them all.

Both Dylan fans, we swapped stories, and after the interview he gave me a tour of the Vegas lights. Then we grabbed a beer at one of the casinos.

Yeah, I love him. A friend of mine, his older brother had all his records. He definitely changed my thinking.

Bob Dylan isn't actually my name. It's not his name either . . . I just liked the way it sounded. And I didn't like the way my other name sounded. The response, the difference was amazing. Just night and day. A lot of times, people'll say, "Give me a song, Bob." What do I do? Depends how I'm feeling.

What *was* my name? I'm not telling. I'm not wanted or anything, but . . . I'm Bob Dylan. I'm secretive.

Grew up in upstate New York. Kingston . . . the first capital. It was burned to the ground by the British, in the Revolutionary War. I was heading for Hollywood to do something in movies or something. But it was too expensive there, so I stayed here. And it's been ten years. I just work in a casino. I count money. A cashier. I'm in a union place but a non-union position. There's crap in both of them, you know—politics, egos clashing, people talking out of the sides of their mouth and everything. But I think the union's a better deal in this city, anyway. That's just my opinion.

The best part of Vegas—well, the colored lights and stuff are nice, but it kind of wears off after a while—you think there'd be all these mobsters, evil people, you know. I mean, there's some of that, but 99 percent of the people are just really real people. They're the friendliest people I ever met in my life, the people I work with. You wouldn't think so with all that pressure. Security is intense because there's so much money, you know. You can't really pick your nose without . . . There's about fifteen cameras on me all the time.

This summer's been a killer so far. My apartment's so warm. I go to the library. Read. Just beating the heat. Thankfully, I work in an air-conditioned place. I just got on day shift recently. Eight to four, or something like that. Yeah, this town never shuts down. All the apartments out here have signs that say, "Keep Quiet 24 Hours," because people work three shifts.

When I first got here, I went to every show in town. There's like no end here. Whatever you want to do. Like I went to the circus two weeks ago, a water park the day before yesterday, fireworks, Fourth of July, baseball game, a show every once in a while. A concert, poetry readings, stuff like that—there's a definite counter-culture presence. Once in a while I go out and gamble. But I never win. It's foolish.

Am I religious? Do you ask all your people this? I don't know. I like what Woody Allen said: "Not only is there no God, but try finding a plumber on weekends." Yeah, I believe in God, but there's so much politics and stuff involved in it now, just such a big show. I think everybody kind of finds God themselves. And the other stuff is good too: Buddha. I'm reading about Buddha and everything. I guess, yeah, I believe in Jesus. I think he's gonna come back. I don't think it will make an awful lot of difference to a lot of people. Probably just like an article in the paper, you know: "Jesus came out of the sky in Jerusalem. Meanwhile, the International Monetary Fund . . ."

My dream? To be Hugh Hefner. Nah, I'm just kidding. I'd like to see the whole world. Travel the world. I haven't really traveled in a long time. I want to see Europe, the Parthenon and all that kind of stuff. Win a million dollars. I don't know.

I've always had kind of a sarcastic attitude. . . things that people take serious, I find humor in. I've lived my life so fully so far. I've seen a whole lot of things and done a lot of things and met a lot of people. I've been around—even though it isn't everywhere I want to be. ■

amelia earhart

Gainesville, Florida
22 years old

I awoke to a solitary dawn on Charlie Chaplin's shrimp boat in South Carolina the morning I was to meet Amelia on her day off. Six hours of Spanish moss–draped highways later, I was walking the streets of Gainesville, surrounded by tan young students.

Amelia answered the door in a crisp charcoal suit with a bright white blouse, wearing heels and expertly made up. I had just been going for the clean look, and I felt the comparison was not in my favor. We sat on the couch in the house she shares with her lifelong best friend and two sorority sisters—all of whom had graduated together from University of Florida the previous year. They walked in and out, occasionally chiming in at Amelia's request for details, opinions, or corroboration.

From the outset, I was struck by her poise, extroversion, and determination. I greatly enjoyed my tour of TV 20 and the opportunity it afforded for a behind-the-scenes look at the work of a talented, aspiring young television journalist.

Actually the best, I guess, pickup line I've ever heard was, "Hey, Amelia, how 'bout you crash at my place later?" (He was joking, he didn't really mean it.) It's a way to meet people, you know? I mean, you would never probably talk to your waiter or waitress more than, you know, "Yes, this is what I'll have . . ." But sometimes if they see your name, they might sit down and have a conversation with you.

My father was a pilot in the Navy. And actually he was asked just as much as I am with the name, "Are you related to Amelia Earhart?" And he would always joke (I promised him to tell you), "Well, I don't really know my mother, I was just born off an island in the Pacific somewhere . . ." They named my sister normal: Whitney Nicole. And then I was a surprise so they were like: I think we've got to do it . . . And he wanted to be able to change his answer. So if someone says, "Oh, any relation?" they looooove to say, "Yes, she's our daughter."

I love attention and that's one thing it got. Especially now that I'm going into news and being in the spotlight. I started working at TV 20 in August. I was on the air by December. It is the most high-stress, deadline-oriented job you could have. Because every minute counts. I love it. *Iiii* love it.

For the past two months I've been working as Amelia Graham—that's my middle name. My news director asked me to change my name. He said he thought that when people would hear "Amelia Earhart," they wouldn't be listening to what I *said*, they would be talking about my name. At the time, I was like, Okay, I need this job . . . I didn't really understand why, because I had worked as a reporter and been Amelia Earhart. And if anything, that got people to talk to you, to open up. But you're never going to

work at one place, in this business, for more than two, three years at the most before moving on and finally settling down in the biggest market that you can. So hopefully the next one will let me use Amelia Earhart.

Gainesville is market one sixty-six. New York is number one. So that kind of gives you an idea. There are a hundred and sixty-five stations between me and New York. And I would love to end up in Katie Couric's seat—I mean, you know, in ten, fifteen years. But more realistically, while that's a goal, I understand even if you work harder than you ever thought you would be able to work, you may not get there. A lot of it's fate, luck, being in the right place at the right time. So, what I do every day is I'm working on my

"Tomorrow is a new day with no mistakes in it." If you don't want to think about what you thought about today, don't. Do something new, do something fresh. There are no mistakes in the future.

résumé tape. When I get off and I did a great job, I grab that thing and put it on my save tape.

Right now, I work the night beat. So my schedule's flip-flopped. I get there at three or four in the afternoon. And there's an assignment editor who says, "Okay, today you are covering . . . ," and you know, it could be anything. Like last night, I covered a True Love Waits rally that promotes abstinence until marriage. Here I was interviewing fourteen- and fifteen-year-olds. The day before, I was covering a County Commission meeting, interviewing people about rezoning. Funny and random things as well as more, like, hard-hitting news.

I'm now a one-man-band, is what they call it. I take the camera and the tripod and shoot all my interviews—frame 'em up, hold the mike up front and stand away from the camera. Then move the camera, do like a wider shot to get both of us in it and me listening, nodding. Then move the camera again when I shoot my standup, which is when I say, you know, "We're here at the High Springs Police Department where at six p.m. tonight Officer so-and-so was arrested . . ." Then I run around the camera and push stop, see how it looks. It's hilarious! Then I try to get back to the station by nine o'clock p.m. So pretty much you log your bites for thirty minutes, write for forty-five minutes, edit for forty-five minutes, and then you're on the air at eleven. A lot of times I go live from locations.

I think I took *Don't Sweat the Small Stuff* to the extreme. I don't worry that much. I can't remember the last time I was nervous. I mean, we're *aaaaall* human. Everyone makes mistakes. I've made them on the air. I made one last week . . . It just sounded so ridiculous and I wanted to laugh, but of course I couldn't, you know, it was the six o'clock news.

I want to report for another six, seven years, and then eventually move into anchoring, when I'm ready to have a family, you know, age thirty-five or so. Anchoring lends to a family much better than reporting does, because breaking news happens and you go.

I'm living with my best friend from . . . life, and two sorority sisters. We all went to UF together. Gainesville has a pretty good nightlife downtown, so it's a lot of fun. I enjoy playing golf. Football season, my family comes up for every game, and my dad and I usually play golf before. I *love* to sing. I love to play the piano. I love scrapbooking. I love listening to music, going to concerts, Broadway shows—*love* that. If I could do anything in my life, it would be to star on Broadway! But I also love to play sports, and I'm really competitive. It's funny but that's a really big part of my personality, I'm really a competitive person. I love to play games. I always said whenever I find my husband, he has to like to play cards!

I always saw my grandmother as just the most amazing person. She was just a *lady,* I mean she exemplified what a Southern woman should be. And I definitely want to end up like her. I'm proud of where I come from. I consider myself very fortunate. First of all that I was given the opportunity to have a great family and then second of all that I have not screwed it up. It's something that takes hard work and communication and calling when you don't have the time.

I don't know, I'm proud of having this job. I'm really proud to go on the air every night and know that this is something that I set out to do and I did it. I want to be something great. And different. Maybe that's where the Amelia Earhart thing comes in, because I truly would love to be remembered like her. I don't know if there's room for two of us, but that'd be great, you know? ∎

What does it mean to be an American? I just think it's amazing. Especially the chances that women have in this country, I know people talk about oppression and how women are still not seen as equals and there's this glass ceiling. I really don't see it. Maybe that's because I have rose-colored glasses, I don't know. Look at Amelia Earhart, she did it. And there is nothing, nothing stopping me.

Be the best that you can be. If you're a ditch digger, you be the best ditch digger there is. If you are an engineer, you be the best engineer there is.

betty ford

Little Rock, Arkansas
54 years old

My Betty Ford interview was, far and away, the highlight of an otherwise lackluster birthday (peeling paint at the Red Roof Inn . . .) in Little Rock. Her neighborhood, her house, her manner . . . all dignified and serene. Her stories about the intricacies of school administration were fascinating. All the more so for opening my eyes to these worlds of remarkable complexity—which exist in each locality across the country.

To my delight, she invited me to visit her school in Conway the following morning to take pictures. This was a real privilege.

I really didn't think about it until after I was married, until I started writing it. I thought: *Betty Ford* . . .

I'm an elementary principal. Kindergarten through fifth grade. Very, very challenging. *But*, I enjoy every minute of it. I don't know of anything else I would have rather done. I think that I'm stern, but I'm fair. I'll tell you what one kid said to a new kid. He said, you never want to go to Miss Ford's office. She's nice, but you never want to go to her office . . .

Both my mom and dad came to Arkansas as sharecroppers. When I was six or seven, my dad bought 120 acres of land and started farming himself. Raising cotton and beans and the whole gambit. Raised chickens and cows and hogs. We all had to work. Six girls and there were four boys.

My mother was not educated, but she always wanted us to have more than they were able to give us. She knew in order for that to happen, we had to get an education. All ten of us were offered the opportunity to go to college. All of us went except three, because they chose not to go.

I worked my way through college. Would you believe I was in maintenance? I helped the custodian clean the administration building.

I'm an outdoor person. I love this time of year. It's humid, but I love it. Wake up in the morning, the birds are singing and the trees and everything is in blossom. I get up at four forty-five so that I can have quiet time meditating with the Lord. You know, Give me the wisdom to know what to say, the courage to do whatever I need to do today. Some mornings I'll get up and have my coffee and quiet time on the deck. It's just absolutely breathtaking.

And then, I'm on my way to work. When I get there, it all starts . . . After all the kids are gone, then I have time to go back to my office,

read and respond to emails, respond to paperwork, reflect on what has happened today, and look at my calendar and think about what's going to happen tomorrow.

On a good day I get home about five-thirty. And that's not often. And sometimes I get home at eight-thirty, quarter of nine. Depending on what time I get home, dinner will consist of a turkey sandwich or a bowl of cereal. I really don't get a balanced meal until the weekend. Saturday is clean house and do laundry. And Sunday, I go to church.

I find the time to run, to walk, or to do a little bit of gardening and work in my yard. I started running in 1980 and I've been running ever since, usually just two miles, and I have exercise equipment in my garage. So I'll run and then I'll work out, probably about thirty, forty minutes in the garage with the exercise equipment. But that's relaxing to me. I think that's how I keep my sanity.

I'm divorced. I live alone—I don't necessarily like that, but that doesn't mean I'm unhappy. I would like to be married again, but if that's in the Lord's will for my life, that'll happen too. I have a twenty-eight-year-old son, who lives in Fayetteville. In '95 I nearly lost him to an aneurysm. But he—thank the Lord—overcame all of that. So that's ultimately one thing that I'm thankful for.

I'm thankful that I have family, and I've always had family support. And, I would say, that I was reared by both of my parents. I'm proud of what I've done in life. I won't say that it was a struggle. I just thought, you know, everybody had to do this in order to get where they want to be in life. We grew up in poverty but we never knew we were in poverty. You know, we didn't have much, but they loved us. And they taught us to work. ∎

What does it mean to be an American? Freedom. To make our religious choices, to choose whether we want to do nothing, or whether we want to aspire to the top. It's available. He knew when He created us, that there would be some better off than others. He talked about the poor you would have with you always. So I guess He, in his divine way, made *Americans* the ones with what everyone else would like to have.

I usually go for the truth, even if it is painful.
I like to know what is real.

greta garbo

Louisville, Kentucky
43 years old

Soft-spoken, candid, and thoughtful, Greta was easy to talk to. She gave me a tour of her cancer research lab in downtown Louisville. In demonstrating the laser work they perform, she unselfconsciously donned bulky dark goggles while talking at the camera. It was a riot to see the cursive "Dr. Greta Garbo" stitched so matter-of-factly on the white lab coat she wore.

We talked in her office, and she showed me some of her own photographs—stunning nature shots she'd taken on trips with her photographic society and natural history group.

If I can help friends, I'll go out of my way to do that. I would say that I'm maybe shy, introvert. In a big group I would probably be silent and not say very much. Some would tell you that I'm not diplomatic, that sometimes I make things difficult for me and for other people, especially here at work. Sometimes it is better trying to play the game, and not trying to make things right or telling what is going on without considering what could be the repercussions of it. That is something that I need to work on.

Garbo is the family name. Actually Garbo means politeness in Italy. Heh heh heh. My father did want to call the firstborn with the name of the actress so he can tell people that it's a relative . . . Similarities? My mom would say the big feet! There are people joking, asking me if I want to be alone. Sometimes I don't like that, because I really don't want to be alone most times. Sometimes I would not want to be noticed, and with a name like that, there is just no way . . . Most of the time it did help breaking the ice. So I really shouldn't complain.

I was born in Italy, near Venice—San Donà di Piave. I studied in Padua and my mother and my brother are still there. I'm worried about my mother, so sometimes I feel guilty not to be there. I came here for a visiting scholar position. Initially I wasn't thinking about staying. But the situation kind of made me stay, and I think now it's a choice. Life is easier here. You have a lot more.

Depending on the day, I run experiments in the lab or a culture. Being that there are a lot of people using laser, we have to kind of coordinate. It's easier for me to stay late than other people . . . I don't have children, six years I'm divorced. I go home and prepare dinner. I usually talk with my boyfriend on the phone. And that is my day.

I like the lab work, but my dream would be to travel and take pictures. I did enter some competition and got honorable mention. I like to be able to see something beautiful and record it with a film to make it a little mine. Kentucky has a lot of beautiful areas and I enjoy nature, beautiful things that are around, art, music, and everything that make people go out from the little problems of everyday life.

In Europe there is a lot more history, a lot more museum, a lot bigger culture. Here sometimes, especially in the very rural parts, it's kind of, missing. Even information. TV is a lot more criticism and there is a more open dialogue and more critical way of looking at things than what happens here. Here it's a lot more presented one way and that will be the only way you know about it.

Will I go back to Italy? It will be very difficult. I will probably not be able to do research there. There is a lot less possibility. Plus at my age up there it would be even too old to find any job. There are so many people that are without a job that they will for sure not hire somebody that is older. Thirty-five years old is like the cut point.

I'm not completely okay here because I miss a lot of things and then the same thing, when I go back to Italy I miss a lot of things that I have here. Really it would be too good to smash them together or to go back to the way it was before leaving, but everything changes, it will never stay the same.

I found a lot of very nice friends, nice people here. They tell me that I should be proud. That it's something that I've been able to be independent in another country beside the language barrier and everything different. That not everybody could come to another country. ■

I see this like the land of opportunity. You really have a lot more chances to make it, economically, at work, than in a lot of other parts of the world. So I think this should be appreciated. People can continue to work, even seventy years old or later on. I notice here that people are religious because they really are convinced. In a place like Italy you have to, otherwise you will have problems. Now maybe things are changing a little, but years ago was like a state of religion where you had the priest coming to school and it was, like, imposed.

What does it mean to be an American? Freedom. That's what America is. I think we're the greatest country in the world. I mean, since 9/11, it's really gotten difficult. It blew me away going to an airport afterwards . . . I had to take off my shoes. They tried to take that away from us, but I don't think they did. My parents sent me to the East Coast for the bicentennial trip, and in '86 I went back for the rededication of the Statue of Liberty. That's the one good thing about that side of the world, how American it is.

Show the aloha spirit. Reciprocity makes the world go around. This is corny, but "the smile on your face is the light in the window that says you're home."

jerry garcia

Honolulu, Hawaii
41 years old

My trip to Hawaii was, start to finish, bathed in what I imagine the aloha spirit to be. Jerry met me at the Honolulu Airport, glorious-smelling tuberose lei in hand. After dropping my gear at my hotel, we headed out to a downtown club in which he holds a "very minority" interest and talked at the bar as he ordered an array of local delicacies, including some fantastic poke. My trip to Hawaii was cruelly brief, but Jerry was determined I'd see as much as possible in my twenty-four hours there. I spent the entire following day with Jerry and his beautiful family. Jerry and I escaped the tourist throngs of Waikiki, stopping at a local dive to grab lunch "plates," which we ate overlooking the crashing surf of a nearly empty beach that was obviously also off the beaten track. Then we went back to the Garcia home to record the interview, meet Terry and the twins, and eventually all head out for a scenic tour, stopping at parks, beaches, and other dramatic vistas. We returned to their home for a casual dinner, and over my protests, Jerry insisted on taking me to the airport for my eleven p.m. flight. When I made my goodbyes, they handed me a goodie bag to remember my journey there! Next morning I was back at LaGuardia.

I liked this shot because the evident gusts of wind helped express the happy hilarity of keeping up with twin baby boys.

The world is full of Deadheads. And that's not a bad thing. I'd get these calls, people asking me if I was *the* Jerry Garcia. Every now and then I'd have to hook one and take 'em along for a ride. My wife didn't like me doing that. But it was kind of funny. Some guys are really dedicated Jerry Garcia fans, and if they think they're talking to the guy, they're in heaven.

I was born in the Texas panhandle. But I lay no claim to Texas, 'cause I was raised in Ruidoso, New Mexico, a resort town up in the mountains. My ancestors from my mom's side were Spaniards. And then on my dad's side, Mexicans, you know, in what was originally Mexico. My father worked his way up from a cotton picker and learned plumbing and then went on to start his own plumbing company. He provided for five kids and taught us the value of work. I'm in the middle, the oldest boy.

I married a hula dancer; my wife used to dance. We've got two beautiful twins. Sixteen months old. Nicodemus Rikkio Garcia and Ezekiel Kazuo Garcia. So you can see the Japanese Mexican mix there. We've been together almost twelve years but still . . . every now and then we find something new about each other's culture. I think that's a big thing in Hawaii as far as what makes this place so unique. I think people in Hawaii are pretty happy because they learn to tolerate each other.

The twins are our automatic alarm clock, up by six-fifteen, six-thirty. We're ready to leave by seven and—thank God—Aunty Irene or my mother-in-law come and watch them and we go to work downtown. I drop off Terry and then I go to my office with Aon Corp. I've been in the life insurance business for the last seventeen years. But my sister and her boyfriend have a home health care agency, and just hired me as Chief Financial Officer.

I pick up my wife again at four and we spend an hour with the kids, either playing, reading books, or going to the park. Start bathing them at six-thirty, feed them around seven, and then put them down by eight. That's the whole day. Catch the ten o'clock news and then back to reality. The weekends, because of the outdoor situation, we like to take them out places.

Nationally, right now I'm real concerned about our approach to world peace. There's I think some guys are a little trigger-happy over there in your neck of the woods. But mostly, I worry about little things you can pretty much take care of, yeah? Just providing for my family is the major number one worry and I don't think that makes me different than 99 percent of the other men out there. Decent men, that's for sure.

I'm a devout Catholic. Practicing. A Republicrat—a registered Democrat, but I tend to vote for who I think will do the best job. I've thought about getting into politics. I've always been a leader. I was president of my professional association, president of the student body in high school. Right now I sit on the Political Action Committee board of directors for the life insurance industry. Not anything glorified, it's just that we give money to politicians so we'll be heard, buy tickets to the fund-raising things and show up.

I pretty much smile all the time. I enjoy life, because I've been exposed to the other side and it's not too pretty. I have two kids and a beautiful wife and I live in Hawaii. There's something to be said about waking up every day and it's a beautiful day. It kind of gives you a different outlook on life instead of waking up and it's all gray. Every now and then that happens just to keep us honest. We'll take two days of this and be on our merry way.

I'd say I've got the world by the hair and I'm pulling it downhill. ∎

Be honest, be true to yourself. Have fun, have fun.

al gore

Globe, Arizona
20 years old

Al Gore was full of energy and curiosity; he talked and moved a mile a minute. He had me meet him at the car wash, which is something of a gathering spot in Globe. We made our introductions as he scrambled around his truck and hosed down his dirt bike in the back. He then drove to the highest point in the area so that we could survey the town of Globe and the copper mines that had put it on the map. A ferocious downpour began, pretty much obscuring the view, but leading to the mud bogging story.

We then headed for La Casita in town, where he held forth over some great enchiladas. As we sat there, he had a number of hilariously direct questions for me, but this is a favorite: "Do you have a social life? Eheh! . . . nooffenseoranything. But I mean is this like, do you make this kind of like your social life or . . . being on the road, that's why I was like, asking?"

I feel funky if I don't get a smile out of somebody. I've always tried to make people laugh. I was voted best sense of humor throughout the high school. Always, always in the principal's office. I always got out of it too! Just smooth talking and bullshit.

I'm a redneck to the bone. I don't look like it I guess, the stereotype redneck or hillbilly, you know, but I am. See, when it rains, my friends will call me: "Hey, dude, let's go mud bog, man." *Anytime* it rains, we'll go see how muddy and how nasty and horrible of a spot we can get our trucks in and out of—just for, you know, just for the hell of it!

I was born and raised in Globe. I've never been out of the state. Big city life was in Phoenix, so I decided, why not try Phoenix? When I moved to Phoenix I actually got a job as a mechanic: *Let's see what you can do from working in the garage your whole life.* I did repairs: engine rebuilds, carburetor adjustments, and little things, you know, new tires on bikes. Not knowing anybody I drove back and forth on the weekends, and my truck, doesn't get, like, squat for gas mileage. So I quit that job. But that job was great, because I rode so many bikes that I never would've got the chance to. I was fascinated by it.

I'm a talker. People personality. For a while I worked nights, and the line I was on didn't let me talk. So that was shifts of doing the same thing . . . in silence . . . And you'd think about, *well, I've got to do this when I get home and in my spare time,* you know. Then by the end of the night, you've thought about everything decent and good in your life . . . *and* all the little bad things. That's the way our minds work, the negatives work their way in and they won't go away. Personally, I need something to my job that's gonna grab me.

I work at TRW. I'm making really good money right now. But I blow money left and right—that's the thing that kills me . . . six grand for a toy that could kill me in a second. It's ridiculous and it's stupid, I understand that, but it's what I like to do. I'm not doing drugs, I'm not out drinking, so give me that, you know. When I was about four, I had cancer, and I guess I feel like I was given a second chance to live and don't need to get drunk and do something stupid.

I'm not going to say *I* started it, but when I first got my bike, nobody hauled their bikes around except for like when they went riding . . . We were riding every day, so we always had them in the back of my truck. Well, everybody started doing that. I don't want to be a trendsetter; I want to be different. I want to have my thing. I don't care about image. Image burns me up.

My mom, I love her to death, but I idolize my dad. He really has not done anything extravagant, or real, real, real productive in his life but raise a family and live an honest life—a good old American small-town boy. Raising his kids the best he can. He has raised me to be as honest as I can, treat myself as I treat people, and live life the way I see fit but yet in a respectful manner.

Growing up my dad was always messing with old motors. He's a builder, an inventor of sorts. Not really like creating something that's never been done, but he'll slap shit together. Right now he's building a 1934 Dodge Pickup from the ground up—with all Ford stuff on it. A Dodge frame and body with a Ford engine, Ford front and steering . . . a Frodge.

I idolize people that do what they want. Want something in their heart and they go for it. ■

What does it mean to be an American? **Free to live your life the way you want to live it. Live your life as good as you can, the way you want, stand up for what you believe in, and do it all legally, if you can.**

43

What does it mean to be an American? I go to Chicago and I think, man, this is America! This is really cool. We got Japanese, we got Polish, we have Mexican, we have Spanish, we have the melting pot of the world right here. What made America great is the hard work ethic of all these different groups getting away from persecution throughout the world. It's those kind of people that came over here. That didn't have the fear. It takes that. That is what's made the United States great.

44

You won't get anywhere unless you're bold and take some risks in life. Life's short. Go for things.

jim hoffa

Newton, Kansas
46 years old

With many of the interviews, I was struck by the fabulous complexity of whole worlds about which I knew nothing. Jim's company, for example, produces customized magnetic equipment, with clients ranging from the auto industry to the emulsion meat industry (think hot dogs).

By the time we'd finished talking in the beautiful home the Hoffas built themselves, it was evening, and Jim invited me to join the family for dinner (which for them nearly always means eating out). They took me to a great old steakhouse so that I'd be able to have some famous Kansas Black Angus steak while in town. Definitely a highlight of the journey.

I'm in sales, and sales people have to do something to be remembered, to be able to get in, and my name really opens up a lot of those doors. If you do a nice job of introducing yourself, whether it be a secretary or whatever, they go, "Oh . . . *Jim Hoffa?*" And the first question out of their mouth: "Are you related?" And I usually say, "Yes, but very distant at the moment," and so all these barriers start falling down. You haven't gotten to the trust stage, but at least you got through the conversational stage.

I am related to Jimmy Hoffa, there's no doubt about that. I don't know if it's seventh or seventeenth cousin, but it's someplace in there. I think there is a lot of likeness, 'cause don't get in my way or I'll run over you. That same determination made him successful. Jimmy Hoffa, a hardnosed guy from down the block, made it the hard way, didn't want to be controlled by anybody—whether it be government, mafia, or whatever.

That's kind of been my attitude all my life. Get in my way and I'll run over you. I don't care how big you are. Even though I am a little guy, I'm going to whip you one way or another. My ornery can-do attitude has gotten me a lot of places in life that probably people would never get. I'm the vice president of marketing and sales and I don't even have a college degree. Not that that's good. But I do things that people with college degrees, masters, doctorates, can't do. And it's because of a can-do attitude. Tenacity, follow-up, honesty, integrity . . .

In my free time, I'm a full-time mechanic keeping my kids' cars running and keeping the tractors running. If I can keep 'em going, you know, then I can afford the school for the kids. I want my children to be leaders. We've had them in a private school, and then they're off to Oral Roberts. Mary and I have both sacrificed, I feel, for their educations. Mary's car's got 250,000 miles . . .

I like to think that I'm the ultimate motivator . . . the team dad. Katie plays tennis. I'll try to travel anywhere she goes to play tennis. I love to watch. I take my little digital camera and I take pictures of them and I root them on, yell and scream . . . I'm very positive.

I grew up a little different to most kids. My dad died when I was, like, seven years old. He owned a factory and there was an explosion. I have one brother, who passed away about a year and a half ago. He was 363 days older than me, we were very, very close. When he was a junior in high school, there was a chemical imbalance in his body—they say that can come on at puberty. That really changed my mother's whole life. He could function and drive, but if he held a job and there was something traumatic that went on, it would set him back.

I'm proud I guess that I could build a house like this. Own a property like this. Proud of seeing my daughters graduate and have drive. Glad that they're going to have the college education that I didn't. I have great kids, I have a good job, I have all these things, but as far as what's inside of Jim Hoffa, who likes that risk and that challenge and that reward and that stress . . . ? It's time to go out on my own, do my own thing, be the boss. My dream is to own my own business. Take the risk.

But you still have to be fiscally responsible . . . and that's the tough part right there. If the kids were through college, it would be a no-brainer. My wife's happy and my kids are happy. I value my family. I'll worry about my own life later. And hopefully this wild kid from Iowa can add a little more value than just his good ol' time. ∎

Whatever you decide to do, try to do a good job.
Always ask, Did I do my best?

oliver wendell holmes

New Haven, Connecticut
63 years old

Nine years ago, I was a student in Professor Holmes's phenomenal history, philosophy, and literature course, Modern Social Thought. I had to smile during our interview when he talked about pushing his students to realize their potential. This is precisely why his class was one of my most rewarding, if sometimes unnerving, undergraduate experiences. While he's an intense intellectual force, Professor Holmes also exudes warmth and has a quick, booming laugh, which erupted when I ventured that I remembered his office as somewhat photogenic . . . They say a clean desk is the sign of an empty mind.

Professor Holmes—or "Ollie"— was named after an uncle who had died. The "Wendell" was given because his father wanted him to become a lawyer one day.

Can you imagine having a name like Oliver growing up in the streets of New York? And, you know, being a black Jew wasn't always easy. Black wasn't always easy! Actually, it provided me with a lot of strength. I was at a Jewish school, and we would go through different hostile neighborhoods. And you were obviously a target, you know, carrying these books . . . I didn't like running home every day, so I took up boxing, at a local club. Learned Judo. And it ended up being very, very helpful. And when someone challenges you and you respond to the challenge, they decide to back off, right? It's the body language.

I came to Wesleyan because I wanted to do more interdisciplinary kinds of history. I teach History of the Humanities and Issues in Contemporary Historiography. So various themes, Hegel and Marx, sort of broader world-type interpretations, and we're using epidemiology as the theme—plagues and diseases. And feminism and post-structuralism, and theories of evolution, so it's a whole range of interesting reading.

The one I'm doing in the fall is French Existentialism and Marxism, so a different sort of mix of philosophy and literature and theory. I teach Tuesday, Thursday schedule, department meetings on Wednesday. So I come four days, usually Monday through Thursday . . . office hours, time to meet with theses—this year I have two. I run a tight ship, particularly because a lot of it's theory and you're dealing with ideas and you want to get on top of it, so that when the writing phase comes, it's not overwhelming.

If I don't have to stay here, I'll pick up my son first, and then the girls. A lot of juggling. Every day. And then it's five, five-thirty, you've got to help get dinner ready and take the dog out . . . If I'm lucky, I can start doing some of my own work nine-thirty, ten o'clock. I'm a night owl. I don't go to bed until two or three in the morning. But that's the only time I get work done.

My wife's an architect. My son is in first grade. My daughters are seniors, so it's been stress city at home. Applying to school. It's horrible. With twins, it's not always a factor of two; it can be sometime a factor of ten. Girls are rough. Adolescent girls. Uch! If I can hang in— they say, by sophomore year—I said, I don't know how I'm going to *survive* until then . . .

But you know, I wouldn't trade it for anything. When they go away . . . I'm gonna hate it. I mean, a quiet house, I just dread the thought. Right now it's filled with decibel levels! But I'm going to miss that, I know.

Worry about? Right now, college. *How am I going to pay for these girls?* It's thirty-six thousand a year, room and board, thirty-six thousand! Horrendous. You know, academic salaries are not great. It's interesting, since my wife's illness, cancer, I have a very different sort of focus. It's not so much a worry as that I reflected on priorities and concerns and things I don't take for granted.

I treat every day as a gift now. Every day as a gift. Lessons I try to instill, as my daughters are becoming more uncertain of themselves and their future, that no matter what obstacles they have, they can't worry about things over which they have no control. Be concerned with things over which you do have control. Material things they can take away from you, but your brain is there. And not to give up.

That was something that I got from my parents. My father got that from his mother, being an immigrant. My Jewish grandmother, my father's mother, comes from Russia. I try to instill this sense of whatever you do, try to excel at it. I even tell my students, you know, you have a lot of promise, now you have to start delivering. You hear about potential—it has to be *realized*. ∎

What does it mean to be an American? I don't know anymore. There was a time I believed very much in the melting pot idea. Our family represents that. On my side, you have the black-white mixture. My wife's father was a Holocaust survivor from Vienna, so, as a European, went in the last boat they could get to China, to Shanghai. And that's where he met my mother-in-law. So, to be mixed, black, white, Chinese, Jewish, you know! It's an interesting kind of dynamic. Since September 11, I found, not that I want to make it a more closed society, but I realize there are dangers to having an open society. How do you protect yourself from being vulnerable without being overly repressive? I'm appalled that they will stop people just because they look a certain way. How can you have an open society when these sorts of things happen? So it's very, very tricky. It's difficult times now.

> Listen, girl, I was born in the Depression, back in the thirties, and them was hard times . . . Did you ever hear of a Hoover hog? A rabbit was a Hoover hog.

herbert hoover

Carthage, Missouri
79 years old

Hoover was my second-to-last interview after a full month and a half on the road. Because of a logistics gamble lost, I'd spent the entire weekend at the Springfield, Missouri Motel 6 giving swimming lessons to two young sisters at the motel pool, watching Law & Order, *and fighting off a fever.*

After pulling into the correct Hoover driveway—there were others on the street—I knocked, but received no answer other than the sound of a television wafting through the screen door. Cupping my hands, I peered in to see an older man reclined in a La-Z-Boy, deep in slumber. Finding gentle rapping of no use, I banged at full force until he awakened and invited me into the kitchen. I soon realized that he had never gotten my letter and had no idea who I was or why I was there, so I explained my project and we began talking. I was charmed instantly by the texture and detail of his stories and the ease and generosity with which he shared them.

A few hours later, having exhausted all pretense for staying, I took my leave. Driving back to Springfield, I was startled by my reflection in the car's side view mirror. Where I'd been weary and propped up only by caffeine upon arrival, my face now blazed with life, invigorated.

What does my average day look like? I'll tell you what: it's dark. I don't have a very good outlook on the day anymore . . . haven't been happy since the wife went away. Only time I enjoy myself is when I'm on the lake, fishing.

Here's what I do every morning: I get up around eight-thirty, nine o'clock. I go to Wal-Mart and I get four big cookies, all different kinds. Some of them got strawberry inside, some of them got apple, some of them got pudding inside them, I get four of them. My grandson works over to the garage, the Village Automart, he works there and when I get there he takes a break. He gets his coffee, we have our cookies. Then I'll maybe go over to the body shop, watch the guys working on the cars over there, and then I go to Senior's. Go down to Senior's and have lunch . . . After lunch, me and my friend that I fish with, they got two pool tables down there and we play pool. We play pool for about, maybe we play four or five games and then he goes home and I come home.

I've got a dish out there. I've got a hundred or so channels on that thing. I get westerns twenty-four hours on that thing. I'll come home and start to watch it, then I fall asleep, just like I did when you came in. Then I get up and take a bath and then if it's bingo night—I play bingo a lot, just to get away from the house. I don't like to stay here of an evening, I like to get out. I go out to dinner or go play bingo. We had a dog track, and me and my lady friend, we'd go up there about three or four times a week to play the dogs . . . They could hear me all over that building up there. I was, "Come on dogs! Come *oooooooon* dogs!" We had a lot of good times out there. Now, when they start running again, I'll be goin' back up there. Oh, I sure will. It'll give me somewheres to go.

Now tomorrow night, I'll be going over to Shiverdecker to play bingo. That only costs forty dollars to play over there. Oh, hon, you can play for ten dollars if you want to, but I like to have paper to play with! Darlin', you get on a roll and you can win every time you go. But if you're not on a roll, you may go a dozen times and not win a thing. Now a friend of mine that I fish with, he quit altogether. It got where when we'd go play, I wouldn't sit with him because I don't like his swearing and what he'd call "these damned old broads, they win all the time and I don't win nothing." Some of the guys I talk to when I'm over there, or some of the women, they say they get tired of sitting home. There's nothing at home to do and they're getting tired of watching TV. And that's the reason I go.

I was born in Hoover's administration, I sure was, Herbert Hoover. You know what my middle name is? Lincoln. I was born on Lincoln's birthday. Twelfth of February. Herbert Lincoln Hoover . . . I'd just prefer to have it something else. I've had quite a time with that name through the years. We moved around a lot, you know, and I was a little bigger than the rest of the kids so they'd always sit me in the back. And the teacher'd say, "We got the president in the class this morning." And here they'd *aaaall* turn around . . .

When I was a boy we used to go to Pentecost church and when I would come home from church, I was so upset and scared—I couldn't sleep at night, because they're holy rollers. You know, Pentecost people are holy rollers. And they'd get up, and run around and jerk, some of them, fall over and scream and holler and yell. When I was a boy I didn't understand that. Now, I do. Yeah. The church is over on Oak Street.

What does it mean to be an American? What do I think it means to be an American? It means everything. I wouldn't want to live anywheres else. 'Cause this is God's country, it is. We would have never won the war if it hadn't been for God. Yeah, I like my country that I live in. Yeah, I do.

That's my nephew down there next door, and I've got my daughter right here in the trailer and I've got my boy right there in the back, and then one right there down the road. And one out by Fidelity. Then I lost one about eight years ago, my oldest girl. Two years after I lost my wife, I lost a daughter. I thought the world of both of them . . .

I'm proud of the time I spent in service. I was a gunner on a 105 Hauser. And you talk about a lucky boy! I had a lot of people praying for me . . . Oh honey, I tell you, the people they left . . . It's terrible. It's terrible. It was awful. It sure was. But I want to tell you one thing, woman, there wasn't a person in this United States that wasn't ready to go out to do what they could back when the war broke out, back in '41. But you will never again see it happen like that. Everybody went to bat, boy. And if they hadn't have, I don't think we'd have ever won this war.

When I come out of the service, I told myself, I'll never take another order. I'm going to be my own man. So I'm going to be a farmer. Well, we were just getting by. And my dad was helping me one day and he said, "Son, I'll tell you what's the matter: you just wasn't cut out to be a farmer." So I went to work at the powder mill. Hercules Powder Mill. And that's the best thing that ever happened to me. I worked there thirty-three and a half years . . . retired in '79. I get a good pension from them right now and I got a good Social Security coming.

Yeah, I retired when I was fifty-nine. I told the wife one day, I said, I'm working harder away from the plant and I'm making more money working for myself than out there and I said, What do you think of me retiring? She said, You've always done what you wanted to do, haven't you? I said, Most of the time. She said, Well, if you want to retire, she said, that's good enough for me. Then I did my own work, hon, nobody will believe the wood that I cut during the wintertime. Nobody will believe it . . . I wish you'd talk to some of the people I used to haul wood to. They were amazed . . . I could have a tree cut up in half an hour. Sure could.

I tell you, hon, life ain't like it used to be. It's just a different attitude that people's got anymore. Years ago if you lived in a community and the people found out that these people down here were pretty hard up, they'd have the rest of the community get together and talk about it and see what we could do about it and see if they would accept a little help. And no, it ain't that way no more . . . I know when times were different, yes sir. ■

What does it mean to be an American? I'm very proud, especially more recently, that I've had the opportunity to grow up in America. That we have a great opportunity here. And, you know, I think a lot of people take that for granted. And unfortunately, you know, these recent changes have made us all think or be more patriotic. I think what it means to be an American is to continue to believe in our Constitution . . . but I think that we all need to, as Americans, we need to support our core values. And maintain them. Don't let them get distorted to the point where you don't have any rights. Just maintain our core values, those and our church values.

**Don't do what other people think you should do.
Do what you want to do.**

rock hudson

North Kingston, Rhode Island
43 years old

Rock and I e-mailed back and forth to set up a time for me to head up to his Cranston Super-Value Distribution Center. He has a comfortable and joking rapport with his colleagues; after we talked in his office, he took me on a (subzero) tour of the warehouse facilities. It was so cold I pretty much lost function of my fingers while trying to photograph him, but this North Dakotan seemed not to notice and wasn't even wearing his jacket.

I'm kind of an oddball. I mean, let's face it, at my age only staying with one company. Years ago I was the norm, and today it's changed. I was working in Fargo, and I had the opportunity to come out to Rhode Island and run this distribution center. And of course flew out—never been to the East Coast—flew out here, took a look around, says, you know, can't be that bad. So came out. The rest is history. This was in '99; it's been about three years. Well, you know, they laugh out here because I share stories about North Dakota . . . you know, I've been stranded in my car, and I've seen the whiteout, and I've had nobody come and help me at all. I mean, that's just part of living there.

Just spending time out of doors, that's what we like to do. Just spend a lot of time with my kids and fishing. We took one of the best vacations—my kids and my wife, they still remember it. We went about eight hundred miles north into Saskatchewan, north of the Canadian border. And we spent a week up there with no electricity or anything. And just had a ball, you know, it was great. I mean, the bears were coming in at night to trash the place. But we fished all week; it was quite primitive up there.

My wife's a hero, she's had to go through an awful lot with my career. I spent fourteen years working the third shift environment, so there's a lot of time when we only had maybe a day together, and of course raising the two boys . . . it was difficult. We have a golden rule at our house. If it's inside, it's my wife's responsibility and mine, and if it's outside, it's totally mine. I don't mind helping indoors. But she does not do outdoor work. She has never shoveled. Never shoveled! She doesn't even have to fill her car with gas. Every week I just make sure I

fill the vehicles. So we have some fun with that one, but that's what it's all about.

My wife, she's her own person and I respect her for that. And she has her opinion about many things in life and I have my opinion. And we truly do have differences, but yeah, we always seem to find that common ground that maintains our relationship. My wife and I have two boys. Actually, they're eighteen and twenty-one. The oldest boy lives in Florida. The youngest boy just recently graduated and he's just messing around right now, figuring out what he wants to do with his life.

Well, actually it's my given name—it was done on a dare. Of course, my mom was like, oh my gosh, we can't do this . . . You'd get weird phone calls in the middle of the night. I'd be lying there, and of course I would carry on a conversation with these people. Because I figured they took the time to call me, I'll take the time to find out what is it they really want to know. As you probably realize, yes, I can chat. And I enjoy it. I still have fun with it today.

The thing I worry about is holding my family together. You know, the questions I ask myself are, What happens if mom or dad passes away? Where are they gonna be put to rest? All these kinds of things, started thinking about this stuff lately, 'cause my dad is a medical mystery. He's a war hero. He's got tons of Purple Hearts and medals and I mean he's missing more parts than he's got and he just keeps going. That's why he retired early. And he says it's the best thing he ever did. I worry about my kids. Worry about their future. You know, I see them working hard, I see them trying to find their—I don't know, their mission in life—whatever it may be. ■

> "Yesterday was history. Tomorrow is a mystery. And today is a gift." I kind of like that. I think it's something to live by. I just try to live every day to the fullest.

langston hughes

Washington, D.C.
29 years old

I almost gave up on Langston. Over the course of fifteen months, it took three or four attempts to finally meet up. Luckily, the D.C. area's home to me, so I visit frequently. In any case, he was always genuinely warm on the phone, and somehow I knew this interview would be well worth the wait. I enjoyed bantering with him and found his rapid-fire words incisive and wise.

Langston received a number of phone calls during our interview, and I particularly liked this snippet I overheard:

"No, I'm having an interview. For real. This lady's writing a book about people with famous names. I'll call you back as soon as I finish . . . Ain't what? No, I ain't famous, man. I'll call you back."

Well, my father was named Langston Hughes, *his* father was named Langston Hughes, and further than that, I really can't tell you. The one question I'm always asked: "Do you know who you're named after?" Shh! Who wouldn't know? I been going through this all my days.

I had another brother named Langston. He got killed. He got shot. I didn't know him as well as my other brothers, because he was across town. So my brothers Chuckie and David, we've been through thick and thin together. We're real close.

I used to call my big brother "old stuff," and his friends'd say, "You going to be happy to get this age." Because I grew up in D.C. and it was . . . wild. I can count a whole lot of people that I've known all my life and sooner or later, one person get killed, two people get killed, three people get killed. The way of life, basically. It's not like maybe suburbs, where you can walk the streets and stuff. You always got to worry about gettin' robbed. Always. If you outside, period. Shoot, thirty years old? I'm happy to be here. Honestly, I thank God to make it this far, in this age.

Like five years ago, D.C. was the murder capital of the world. Now, it's low-*er* than it was. More people got jobs and more people got money in their pockets and they ain't got to do this and that to get money any more. That drug game and all that. But now that there's a recession I think it will increase, most definitely.

My father, he started messing up. So . . . he moved out. I was about fifteen, I think. You know, ghetto drugs and stuff. Even though I still seen him, but it wasn't like he was no father *figure* anymore. I wish he would have gotten his self together. But I've been handling stuff like that all my life.

My mother only lives ten minutes away. My daughter lives with her mother. She's twelve now and her little mind acting funny—the teenage thing. I worry about that. My son, Langston Hughes, he'll be ten months. And my fiancée has two daughters, six and four.

My fiancée, she's a good girl. She a family girl too. See, that's what I like. If I wouldn't have met her, I probably still wouldn't be involved with nobody. It'll probably slow me down a lot. Probably help me. I don't hang in the streets like I used to. I think I set an example for a lot of my buddies, being as though I've chilled out, settled down, so-called. And they still on the player thing.

Basically, I go to work and come home to the family. I'm a mechanical engineer at the Hospital for Sick Children. I'm not the type that can stay in the house all day, look at the TV set. I can't even sleep late! I *got* to get outside and get some air. And when I'm outside, I talk to my friends, mess with my cars. I love gadgets, stuff that I can make work. I get something new, I don't know how to leave it alone.

I'm going to school to get a higher license. Four years left. Now I've got my third-class D.C. license. I can go anywhere with that, but wouldn't be *chief* engineer. I'll be finished in a minute though. But! Once I'm finished I'll probably go back. I plan on going to school all my life. I mean you can never learn too much.

I'm happy. Satisfied, no; but happy, yes. I don't plan to be satisfied. I need to do more things. And if you get satisfied, they won't get done.

I've got the dream that everybody else has: I don't want to have financial worries at all—me *or* my family. Big house. All the kids running around. I'd rather the kids grow up in somewhere other than D.C. Not *country* country, but somewhere a little more slower. Not too far from D.C. I love D.C. ■

What does it mean to be an American? I think it's a good thing as far as how other people live in other places. But you know, it's one of them things that you probably don't know what you've got till it's gone.

What does it mean to be an American? Real good base-ball game, real good blue-grass festival. Having a bon-fire in your backyard. Riding an old American-made motorcycle, driving a German car . . . I don't like having to pay taxes on my land and, you know, having to buy a dog tag, it's ridiculous, things like that. But, there ain't a better country in the world. I'm proud to be an American. Yep.

> I don't lie, I don't steal. I drink a little beer and cuss a little bit. I try to treat people decent, try to be a good feller. I'm good to my dogs.

jesse james

St. Marys, West Virginia
43 years old

When I called Jesse James (aka Randall Jesse), he invited me to the bonfire they were having in the yard on Friday evening. I arrived at dusk and snapped this shot in front of the tool shack just before we lost the light. We then sat around the kitchen table with his wife, Trish, and niece, Ralphie. "Show her your room," Trish said, as Ralphie whispered, "He collects everything . . ." The room looked like an antique shop, with glass cases full of all kinds of historical and other such curios. Likewise, their home had been in her family for generations (I saw the original deed) and was filled with beautiful and significant pieces, the history of which he knew in detail. All this, and he was refreshingly down-to-earth.

When we wrapped up the questions, Jesse said, "I don't know if you're in hurry, but we're going to have a wiener roast after a while. Have you ever had a weenie on a stick, you little city girl, you?" How could I refuse? We sat around the bonfire talking until it was late. Though they offered to put me up for the evening, I had to make headway south for the next interview, so I pushed on. They called the next morning to make sure I'd gotten on safely.

Trish said it best: "He's a good-hearted soul."

My grandfather James was the sheriff of Elizabeth, West Virginia—back then it was Work County, Virginia. The farm was in the family until the '60s. Trying to scratch out a livin' on a hillside. My dad said he joined the Navy so he could get the hell off that Work County farm.

My dad was the smartest man I ever knew. Loved string music, hillbilly music. He used to take me when I was a little kid to see all them old bluegrass musicians. Bill Monroe and Lester Flatt. Said Congress should've passed a law forbidding Roy Acuff to die. He said, "Before I die, I'd like to hold a pistol to Perry Como's head and make him sing hillbilly music."

I like to collect books on the James boys. Just rootin' around, going to antique stores and flea markets. I collect all kinds of things. See, here's a Ouija box with the Cleveland Indians on it—I'm a big Indians fan. Here's a poster of Frank James. He was a overbearing, pompous, cigar-chewing know-it-all. Right there's a Harley Davidson dishtowel I almost promise you you'll never see. And the Woodstock poster's original. There's a Jesse James mirror (my dog stepped on it). My grandpa James, he made that book cabinet. That's the flag that was on my dad's casket. Buried with full military honors, twenty-one gun salute, taps . . . shooh! Tore me up. Still does.

Old dad was at Pearl Harbor. He was on the *Saratoga* and the *Yorktown* and the U.S.S. *Henry Berg*. The *Henry Berg* was sunk. He got off it with nothing but the clothes he had on. Henry Berg founded the Humane Society in New York. The dog catchers used to get paid by the head, and they'd lower a big cage into the East River and drown the dogs.

In '83 we bought an old Harley. And it had a sidecar on it. So the first place we went was to my grandma's. She's sittin' on the front porch and I say, "Hey Nanny, you want to go for a sidecar ride?" "Well sure," she said, "I haven't rode in a sidecar in sixty yeeeears!" Little white-haired lady. Raise it up in the air, she'd just grin. Yeahhh, she was a good woman. I bought her an alligator once. She'd hide it behind her back and then she'd come up to you and hold it out there and it'd bite you—it'd bite the blood out of you— and she'd just holler and laugh . . . She had nine kids and she was pregnant for the tenth when the cow kicked her and she lost it. Um hmm. Real country. But I got shoes on . . . and they match! And I've never been married to my cousin.

I'm a truck driver. Crescent and Spraig. I get up at four-thirty, and I work always an eight-hour day, usually more. I get my truck in Marietta, do my paperwork, and I'm outta there by six-thirty, seven. It's a pretty good job. Good benefits— they've been in business over a hundred years. And I got a brand new International. Air-ride seats, air conditioning, yeah, a nice truck.

I worry about finances. We're not poor, but, you know, I worry about my mom. She's got Parkinson's and she's got arthritis . . . about my wife, she's got to have a hip surgery . . . about my dogs gettin' run over out front. You know.

I voted against George Bush. I think he's a dangerous man. Look at the mess we're in now. I voted for Bill Clinton. I voted for Ross Perot. I thought Jimmy Carter was a good president. That's enough about that.

I'm proud to be one of the James boys . . . I'm proud of my house. I'm proud of my dad. I love my dogs and string music. I like to tell a joke . . . have a good time. I like my buddies—bunch of good ol' boys I've known a mighty long time. Got a good woman. Yeah, pretty good life. Happy as a clam. ∎

When you're younger, you have all these great ideals of how it should be. And when you get older, you take a bunch of hits here and a bunch of hits there, and things change and you become more realistic.

thomas jefferson

Wheatland, Wyoming
49 years old

Mostly they just say, "Gee, I thought you were dead." Or, "You look so young for your age." That kind of stuff. I mean, it's probably better to be named Thomas Jefferson than Elvis Presley . . .

I was born in Cheyenne, but my dad was in the Air Force, so we moved around. Growing up on an Air Force base in California, we were just all thrown together. Our next-door neighbors were black a lot of the times and we grew up playing together and there never was any difference. I don't know if it was because we were all economically the same, our fathers were all the same rank, it just seemed normal. And then you come to a place like this and most of the people have never known a black person. I mean, a big trip might be to Cheyenne once a year.

I always thought, you know, like when we were younger, we were going to change the world. But we didn't. The society as a whole is more liberal—there're some people that think that's bad, and some of it probably is (I'm one of the few liberals in the state). But on the whole, it's probably better than it was thirty years ago. In my age, it was the Kennedys, Martin Luther King, John Lennon, Muhammad Ali . . . It's strange out of all those people there's only one alive. Everybody else got shot. After John Lennon was shot, I became a little more pessimistic . . . You know, sometimes I think there really are bad people in the world. Maybe they're just homo sapiens and not human beings. Masquerading around in human bodies.

During the summer, I usually go to the farm by seven, seven-thirty. It's about twenty miles south. Do the farm stuff maybe till five-thirty, six, come home, do gardening, that kind of stuff. See what the stock market did today—got interested in that last winter. Been in an invest-

ment club for probably fifteen years and I'm probably the worst member. Oh, and my wife's a CPA, so she's been more interested, but I never have taken much interest in money—I don't even know how much I make. I'm sort of shocked that I have this, I really am.

You know, I never thought that I would be a farmer. I went to college. And then, '74, the war was over, I had seven hours to go on my Poli Sci degree but, you know, *what am I going to do with that?* . . . I didn't want to be a lawyer. So I dropped out of school. Worked in Laramie for a while. When I got married, my wife's father had a farm out here and he asked if I wanted to try farming, I said, yeah, maybe . . . Stuck here ever since! Wheat farming. Just your typical family farm . . . I don't live to farm, I just farm to live.

I always thought that you just sort of grew up and became something. I thought it was more fate, I guess. But you can actually tweak fate a little bit. I try to teach my kids that you can decide what you want to be. And what you decide to do when you are young affects what you can do when you're older. Whitney, our oldest one, just graduated from UW. She's gonna be a teacher: special ed and elementary ed. So she's off to get a job. And AJ, my son, just joined the Navy, so he's in boot camp right now. And Sarah, she's gonna be a senior next year. She wants to be a doctor. Yeah, they're a pain in the butt sometimes, but once they go away, to not be able to say, you know, what's going on . . . it's strange.

I don't worry about the apocalypse or anything. Mostly the kids. The farm and kids. I think of myself as a pretty decent human being. I never was win-at-all-costs. I sleep pretty well at night. ∎

I enjoyed sitting down with the mellow, thoughtful Thomas Jefferson in his immaculate home. We swapped sob stories about online investing—though he'd fared better than I—and talked some good liberal politics. I particularly appreciated hearing his "lessons learned."

When I came back through town to shoot his picture, I got to meet his wife and son too.

What does it mean to be an American? Boy, you know, it probably means whatever you want it to mean. I think if you're an American you should enjoy everybody around you. And not want to be closed in with the same type of people: "Celebrate Diversity." That's what works best. You get a bunch of different ideas—I mean, you don't have to agree with everybody, but you should be able to listen to other people. Through it all then, usually the best way comes out. It's usually a blend, a compromise. And it's usually fairly good. If you're an American you should recognize that. I do believe that it's the best country on the planet. The best experiment so far. Certainly it could be better. And maybe hopefully through evolution maybe we will be. We can hope.

59

Be responsible for your own actions. Actions get reactions.
Don't live an extravagant life without looking for tomorrow.

helen keller

Wrangell, Alaska
44 years old

When I first spoke with Helen, I ignorantly asked what the best way to drive there was. She started laughing. Wrangell is a thirty-mile island along coastal southeastern Alaska. She was as amused at my name as I was at hers, since she works in Ottesen's hardware store. And though we visited Dorothy Ottesen in the hospital together, we were unable to figure out a connection. The people I met seem to have an open, no-nonsense sort of friendliness.

It was my first trip to Alaska. Although it was absurdly short, Helen took me to see a number of area highlights, and we picnicked at one of Helen's favorite spots "up the road." Coastal Alaska is striking, with masses of land rising gracefully out of the sea. While the fog that hung on for most of my visit cut down on visibility, it enhanced the landscape's natural drama.

One point of clarification: when Helen refers to "the south," she is talking about the continental United States.

California's as far south as I've gone. The south is so much of a rat race. I drive on a freeway and I freak. I mean, there's so many people, you bump into people. You smile and say hi and they look at you like you're crazy. And the smog, the fog, and the funny-smelling air . . . I mean, here it smells the same all the time, unless you're behind a boat or a car. You can drive the street in Wrangell and everybody is waving. You have the one-finger wave or you have the nod. Everybody knows everybody and it's just real friendly.

I'm related to half the town. See, my dad is half Tlinget. His mom was of course full. I'm a quarter. Then Brandy, her dad's a quarter, so that makes Brandy a quarter. A lot of the *native* natives, like my dad, have stayed here.

My family is a hardworking family. We're a fishing family. Started out commercial halibut fishing for my dad when I was sixteen. He's seventy-one, and when it's rough out and really, really snotty, everybody else'll be anchored up and he will be out there. He loves the water. Steve and I both will do it with my dad until he decides to quit. We just all work so smooth together.

After Steve and I met, I asked him, what were his thoughts about getting into fishing—coming from North Dakota and flatland. He said, well, we could try it. So we started gill-netting on this little tiny little twenty-eight-foot bow-picker. Steve, Brandy, and I, we all stayed on this little boat for about four and a half months, into the fall where it started getting real, real cold. When the prices started diving for fish, we sold out of the gill-netting and we ended up deciding to get in the charter business. For all the work, we really weren't making that much money, so we sold our yacht, last year in August.

We'll be together seventeen years, been married fifteen years. I was married twice before . . . right out of high school, when I was eighteen, stayed married for two years. And then I married Brandy's dad and I was married for four years. He actually works with Steve down at the boat shop and they get along fine. Steve said he traveled thirty-eight states to find a Helen Keller to marry.

Steve and I, we just do everything together. We hunt, we fish. We usually try to find one day out of the weekend just to go out and play. Usually we're in the boat going to a cabin or going up the river, driving out the road, it's beautiful. I guess that makes for a closer relationship.

Hunting is my favorite. And this year, I drew an elk permit, so I'm all excited about that. Everybody all of a sudden has been offering me all these guns. I think they want some elk meat . . . I just love the outdoors. I can't get enough of it. I guess my ultimate goal in life is to not work, and spend a lot of time outside . . . I'd like to be able to sit out in the wilderness and paint something, teach myself how to paint.

I'm proud of Brandy. She's going to school in Portland in nursing. And then she's going to go for her master's.

Proud of the fact that we've, that Steve and I have been able to accomplish what we have in our life. We've worked hard.

I worry about Steve's health and my family, their health. I worry about Brandy being down south and being around all the, you know, it's a totally different world, it's a fast world.

Money would be nice . . . but the best thing? I want a grandchild. I mean, not right now, but in the near future. And I would like to see that happen before something happens to my dad and my mom. I think they'd love that. ∎

What does it mean to be an American? You know, a lot of people, they think of Alaska as being cold and dark and whatever, and people are native and whatnot. People seem intrigued with my fishing life. They want to hear all the fishing stories where, you know, the boat almost sinks or something like that. But as far as being a person, I don't think I'm any different. I don't live any different.

> You might not like everything I do. You might not like me as a person, but you've got to love me. 'Cause that's what Jesus said.

grace kelly

Mobile, Alabama
76 years old

"Could you eat a little piece of cake? It's called gooey butter cake," Grace Kelly coaxed (unnecessarily). It was out of this world. I happily settled into the sofa, basking in Southern hospitality, and listened to Grace's stories of the pre-electricity days of country Alabama and life as a pastor's wife, and her reflections on contemporary society.

When we finished going through my questions, she said she wanted me to meet her husband, James, who told me, "I usually refer to her as Princess Grace Kelly. She really is a princess. My wife has given me the best support that any person could ever hope for. She never once complained in all these years. She might have thought about it. In fact the old saying: She never has thought about divorce; she thought about murder two or three times. But she's just that kind of a person. If I ever miss her at church, I can find her right in the middle of a group of ladies. Good mother. Tremendous cook . . . In a nutshell, she's just tops."

I've *tried* to be the best pastor's wife I could be. When my husband first started preaching, I was so afraid he wouldn't do things right. That he'd hurt somebody's feelings or somebody would say something bad about him. I started having migraine headaches. I finally decided he was not going to be able to please everybody. Didn't make no difference what he did. Now I haven't had one since back in the seventies.

He's one of the go-getters, you know. He isn't happy unless he's preaching every Sunday. He retired, but he fills in when they get without a pastor. By him just being an interim pastor, I'm not required to be at as many things as I used to be—or expected, not say required, but expected to be there. Lots of times I force myself to go when I really don't feel like it. Because I'm expected to be there. A big responsibility, but it's soooo much joy.

I can't keep up with him. He's always said, Aww, you're just as old as you feel. I told him, well, I was beginning to *feel* old!

We were both from the same little town, Greenville, Alabama. I was going to what Methodists call a singing school right across the street from where my husband lived, and he was outside working on his car. My aunt asked him if he was going. He said, "Well, I hadn't thought about it." But we hadn't got sat down before he came over and sat down too! So that's the way we started dating. I was not quite sixteen. We got married when I was, like, a month being eighteen and he was nineteen. So. Fifty-seven years in August. We're still together and still love each other very much.

See, I was Grace Parker. And I married my husband, who's a Kelly. At the time, I didn't even know about Grace Kelly. See, it was a little bit after we got married you began to hear a lot about Grace Kelly . . . It's been fun. I've been told many times that I was just as pretty as she was.

I'm the kind of person that if I'm sitting down watching television, I'm halfway reading or I'm doing something with my hands. I'm an avid reader. And I like to do handwork. I'm in the process right now of making a quilt—this is my third one. Takes me a year to make the kind I make. And I have three grown children and nine grandchildren. And three great-grands! I'm really proud of my family and the relationships that they have with us.

I worry that the traditional family-orientated life with man, woman, and children is just going away. Nothing seems to be wrong any more. It's perfectly acceptable to have a child out of wedlock. It's perfectly acceptable for a man and woman to live together not married, woman and woman living together. It's getting where people that attend church don't think there's anything real wrong about it. And it did not used to be that way, nooo . . . Our morals have just really gone down.

We've seen it change. It's harder to get people to come to church. It's harder to win people over now than it used to be.

And it's harder to go out and make personal contact because people don't want to be bothered.

Our whole world is in such a turmoil now. It's so upsetting, isn't it? Life doesn't mean anything to people anymore. There's a killing every time you turn around. We were robbed a couple years ago, out there in our driveway. Now you don't dare leave the door unlocked even in the daytime. I don't see how things can keep going like they are.

I'm of the opinion that if God says it's wrong, it's wrong. There needs to be a renewal back to the things that really matter. ■

What does it mean to be an American? It means everything to me. No other place has the opportunities and the freedoms that we have. I'm so proud that this is where I live. And for something to happen like happened September of last year just blows your mind. But I'm so thankful that we have not had all the wars and things that the other countries have had. We can live peaceably with each other. We can worship as we please.

63

jackie kennedy

Magee, Mississippi
63 years old

When I called Jackie Kennedy, she tried to dissuade me from interviewing her, protesting that her life was boring, joking that she was so ugly she'd break my camera, etc. I swore I'd be passing right by Magee anyway, so she finally, and unenthusiastically, agreed. But when I arrived at the appointed hour, she came to the door beautifully made up, and we had a wonderful conversation in her living room over coffee served on elegant china.

For all her bluster, it's perfectly evident that she's solid gold. In addition to her strength and spirit, I was touched by the tenderness with which she spoke of her late husband, LD, and her grandchildren and children.

I'll always be grateful for the e-mail she sent me after the World Trade Center attack:

I HAVE WONDERED A LOT ABOUT YOU AND YOUR BOOK. HOPE YOU WERE NOT IN THE PART OF TOWN THAT THE TROUBLE IS IN. HOPE YOU ARE OK. LET ME HEAR FROM YOU.

The only advice I've got is to be independent, be yourself, and get out there and show people you can be as good as they are. Nobody's better than nobody else. My dad always told me it don't matter who, nor where, nor how much money they got, nor how they're dressed. You're as good as they are.

We were farmers. We had to pick cotton. That was hard days, back then. People just don't *know* if they didn't live back in them days—it was hard. I can remember when we used to only get a new dress when we had revival, when you started back to school and when Daddy would take the first bale of cotton to the gin, we would all get a new dress. But, you know, we could get by on a lot less. My first job that I had when I got out of high school was at an insurance office. I worked for seventeen dollars a week! Now you get that much in a few hours.

I work at Lee's outlet. I'm just a sales clerk. Well no, I don't guess I like it, but I kind of have to work some. Since LD died, I can draw his Social Security, and you can work if you draw Social Security—thirty-two hours a week. I ended up working too many hours year before last and had to give some back. Five hundred dollars I had to give back! I thought, 'Gollll-ley, I can't believe you're doing that.' Well, I've always been a workaholic. My mom was the same way: forty hours a week until the day she died. She was eighty-two years old, the oldest lady that was employed in Magee.

I've always told my girls, 'Get out and go to work. Work, show these men you can make it on your own.' My first husband told me, 'You will never leave me because you can't make it on your own.' And I guess that was one of my stubborn points. I was determined I was going to show him that he could not control me, that I could make it on my own, and I did. When I moved out from his house I had a hundred dollars to my name and I rented a place and I lived and I've worked every day since.

When LD and I first got married I was working at the finance company and I called people to collect and I would leave my name. You know, it stunned them: 'Jackie Kennedy's leaving a message on my machine!' Oh Lord, until they all found out, it was fun!

I'm a member of Pewter Baptist Church . . . Yes, I'm Southern Baptist. I guess that's what keeps me going. It seems like if you don't go to church on Sunday, the next week is just a mess. I don't know that I guess that has nothing to do with it, but I was raised up to go to church. My daddy seen that we were in church every Sunday. I've tried to do the same with my kids . . . You just try to teach them the best you can. If they follow you, okay. If they don't, there's nothing you can do but pray about it.

I have four kids and one stepkid, twelve grandkids, three great-grandkids. When we all get together now, it's about twenty-five of us. On my days off I make lunch and I put it on the stove and there's kids coming in and out of the house all day long. I just leave it open and they just come and eat. On everybody's birthday, we try to get together, all of us. We have a birthday just about every month except August. I don't know if you love your grandkids more than your kids . . . I tell you, you love them all about the same. Just about. Even the great-grandkids, you get so attached.

My biggest dream would be that I could find somebody that I could love and share the rest of my life with. I don't have this thing about big houses or fancy things. I'm just an old country girl. It don't bother me that my sister has a big ol' pretty house to live in—I used to have one too, years ago. But it wasn't that important to me. I really don't need this big of a trailer. It would mean more to me to have somebody to live with to love that would be good to my kids, like LD was. If I could just find another LD. That's my dream. But I know that's not going to ever happen. So I'll just make myself satisfied with what I have. ∎

What does it mean to be an American? Gosh . . . I guess I'm just proud to be an American. I'm proud to be a Mississippian too. I guess everybody else feels the same way about their town, their country. I'm happy with mine. I don't guess I would change anything. I'm just proud to be here. Proud to be alive.

Be yourself and be honest with people. Your integrity and your ethics are the two things that are gonna either make or break you. And don't ask for handouts.

john f. kennedy

Dover, Delaware
54 years old

I mean, I liked him, I thought he was a good president, and I would have liked to have seen what happened had he been able to fulfill his term. I'm not particularly of that political persuasion . . . but I did think he had a vision. The first president or political leader I remember that I think had a vision.

I was in the Philippines when I was in the Air Force and he was their hero. I mean, people would do things without charging me just because my name was John Kennedy. Because they felt so good about him. Still today, "Oh, you're kidding me," you know. When they see my credit card there's always a comment, even today.

I'd probably be classified as a Republican. But I'm more of a capitalist. I believe in the capitalist system and I'm not very much on socialism. I mean, I just think that people have an opportunity to make their own deal. I did. I knew that if I wanted to go to college, I was gonna have to pay for it myself or get someone to help me, and Uncle Sam was available—for a four-year commitment. So when I got out of the service, I went to college and Sharon worked and supported us.

Well, I don't know what the order would be, but I'm proud of the kids, our marriage, and our financial success. They're good kids, both very smart, never had any problems academic-wise. Scott's to the right of Rush Limbaugh and Heather is left of Bill Clinton—the interesting thing was to have them even out. We've been married thirty-two years and never had a fight. Never thrown anything, never yelled at each other. Thirty-two years. And we didn't buy things unless we knew we could pay for 'em. I think we got that from our parents. We don't cause people problems, we live pretty quietly.

State Farm took me on in 1973. It's been a good employer. I'm an agency field executive. I work with about thirty-two agents in the field. We help the agents train themselves and their staff, introduce new products, and find out their needs and then point them in the direction of a product. I worry about my job—and there's no reason for me to do that. I guess because I always want to make sure I do it right every time. In order to grow, you have to make mistakes. And I don't like to make mistakes. So I probably don't take as many risks as I should.

We get up at six o'clock and walk the dog a couple miles. And I'm usually in the office by eight, eight-fifteen. It's just about a mile up from here. I usually try to be home by six-thirty. And then dinner, the six-thirty news. Then I go to my office in the back of the house and update my portfolio and work on whatever I brought home in my satchel. I've taken a lot of courses to continue to develop my knowledge of the industry, so I study at night a lot of times. Usually nine-thirty, I come back out. That's been one of my flaws during my career, I never just put it aside.

On weekends we go to the beach, we have a place down at Bethany. Normally we just go and vegetate. I'm not a big social person. Most of our social activity was when we had the children still home and State Farm activities—and we've had quite a few of those, we're fortunate. And then I have the Harley Davidson that I just purchased in April, and I really enjoy that. In the fifties and the sixties, Harley Davidson motorcycle riders didn't necessarily have a very good reputation. Now they're becoming very popular—you've got everybody, doctors, lawyers, priests, guys like me that are riding these things, and just enjoying it. I can go out at seven o'clock at night, after I eat dinner, go for an hour and spin around the countryside. And it really relaxes you. ∎

We enjoyed easy and candid conversation—particularly about market and social forces—in the Kennedy home in a quiet suburban Dover neighborhood. After we shot a number of photos in his State Farm shirt, John was a great sport about donning his Harley gear and getting the bike out for this picture. And I've appreciated his emailed words of update and encouragement since.

What does it mean to be an American? Well, for me it means being able to be in control of your own life. Having opportunities that people in other countries don't have, either because of the political system or because of the economic environment that they're in. I mean, hell, we live in the best times we've ever had. Now some people would dispute that because of some of our moral problems and issues, but as an individual you control that. If you stay within certain parameters, then you can do about anything you want. I worry a little bit about the country. Our political process is, I think, close to broke. We need to fix it. People are making their decisions on how to vote over sound bites. We're very gullible people.

Mama always said, respect and kindness go a long way.
I ain't no saint or nothing, but I try to do right by people.

martin luther king

Savannah, Georgia
37 years old

Martin generously met with me on two separate occasions and was truly gracious. He met me at the entrance to his apartment complex—so I wouldn't have to wind all the way back to his place in confusion—and when I accidentally pulled down his blinds while trying to open them for some more light so that I could get a photo of him under the Malcolm X and Martin Luther King pictures he has on his wall, he made me feel like it was nothing at all (though I heard the sounds of hammering as I drove away).

Martin endured my taking photos both at home and at the kidney dialysis center. I was totally impressed by his empathy, self-knowledge, and wisdom. And I've read and reread this interview many times because I find his words so inspiring.

That name does have its moments. I don't care who I come into contact with, if I tell 'em my name, the first thing I'm gonna get is a smile like, Man, why don't you quit playing with me or whatever, and this and that. I have to pull my license out more than a little bit . . . My daddy named me. He liked to hear him talk in his day, that's all. They had pictures of him in our front room in an old, old frame—Martin Luther King and John F. Kennedy and his brother. I'm proud, I'm glad with it, I mean, I ain't name myself but I'm glad I got the name, 'cause like I said, my daddy must be knowing what a powerful name when he gave it to me.

I've been on dialysis nineteen years now. It's mostly like giving blood, it's just a lot longer than giving blood, sometimes three and a half hours, three hours, three fifteen, you know. Three times a week . . . Tuesdays, Thursday, and Saturdays. Just sitting there, like I said, dialysing, getting your blood clean and stuff. . . It's basically doing the stuff that a kidney don't do no more.

But it's all up to what you do on the outside when you leave dialysis. I mean, the biggest job is taking care of yourself. Like I said, I get my treatment and I try to be careful with food. You think about transplant. Yeah, I'm still in a waiting list. But I honestly and truly believe, anything that's meant for me to have, I will get. And the Lord ain't gonna put no more on you than you can bear. I mean, it's hard, but it make a better person out of you and make you realize more about life. And how precious life is.

I have my little moments, but if I feel myself getting in a mood, I go play with my cute little nephew or something, I try to do something, like take a walk, 'cause like I said, life is too precious. I mean, you never know when. It can get

worse. So I don't try to get in no mood, 'cause you dwell on something too long, all it do is it gonna put you down and down and down. And that can make you feel worse than being sick.

I used to worry and be scared of a lot of things, but honestly, so much that happened around me in my life that I'm not even trying to worry no more. What's the use of praying and asking the Lord to look after you if you're going to worry? I learned to try and be as careful as I could about life. I ain't want no party scene. I like to have fun and all that, but I ain't in that position to be taking no kind of chances no more . . . so when it starts gettin' wild, they done lost me, so it's time for me to go. I don't try to judge nobody. I just live the best that I can. Only Martin can answer for Martin.

I'm gonna tell you the truth: when I was coming up I never was a bad kid or none of that, but the people I'd hang around with, they've been in trouble a lot. I could have been jailed, dead, or whatever. I think that sometimes we get the road we travel down for a purpose. You might have something that'll hold you back but still, you make your life the better. After I got on dialysis, I met certain people that really showed me that life could be whatever you want it to be. I met my best friend when I got on dialysis. And ever since we met we ain't never been apart till he passed. So now me and his sister real close. Like I say, you meet people in your life that you never know that you'll meet.

I cannot describe enough how much, I don't think I would have been the same person if I wouldn't have never started going to the Kidney Foundation programs and events and stuff they have. Because I was very—I mean, like, come home, don't do nothing, just sit around the house, whatever. It just showed there's more to

What does it mean to be an American? Last year—that should have made everybody realize how important to be an American is. I mean, people helped total strangers, people they didn't know or whatever. When I say heroes, I mean people like that. That's what a country should be.

life than just like, you know, feeling sorry for yourself.

I go out and drive a van. I can stay home, but I like what I do. It helps me a lot by staying busy too because I don't have time to be worrying, wondering about this and that. Keeps my mind occupied. And you meet different people. I've been 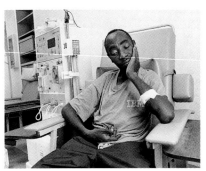 doing this for about five years now, just, like, driving and picking up people in the daytime. It ain't the pay. I mean, I tell my mama and them all the time, it ain't the pay . . . I've been on the other side of needing a ride to go somewhere, when you come home from a doctor's appointment and you got to wait *hours* . . . So I know what they're going through. Nobody should have to sit and wait when they're feeling bad. So now that I am in a position to take people around to doctors, I try to make their day, go by the store for 'em or whatever . . . Everybody should have somebody to check in on 'em, and some you come in contact with don't have nobody. When they go home, they don't have no family; they might have family, but family don't come around and see them. I do not like to see nobody suffering, and they hurt, you know. So I try to do the best I could when I'm out there.

My last stop mostly every day be at Mama's house. Every evening, everybody go out to my mama's house. It's gonna be at least six or seven people there—my little niece and nephews and my grand nephew and then my sister. The neighbors come sit in the yard. And yeah, we play dominoes or whatever and sit around. And I sit there for a couple hours. Sometimes I just stay over. We've never been too far apart because the knit of the family, we kind of stay around each other a lot. 'Cause my mother, well, she lost three kids. It made us come together in some kind of way, because we're up here at my mama's house more than a little bit—mostly 365 days of the year.

Hopes and dreams? I would like to see how my family would have been if everybody would have been around. I mean, just to see the look on my mama's face to see what kind of family she would have had. That's the biggest thing I'm wanting to see, was how my family would have turned out to be.

I mean, I want some stuff but . . . I'm just simple. So long as I have my health and strength and able to come and go. People don't know how lucky it is to be able to do for yourself, how much a blessing it is to get up and just do for yourself. I would like to see other things, to be able to go places. But like I say, one day at a time. ■

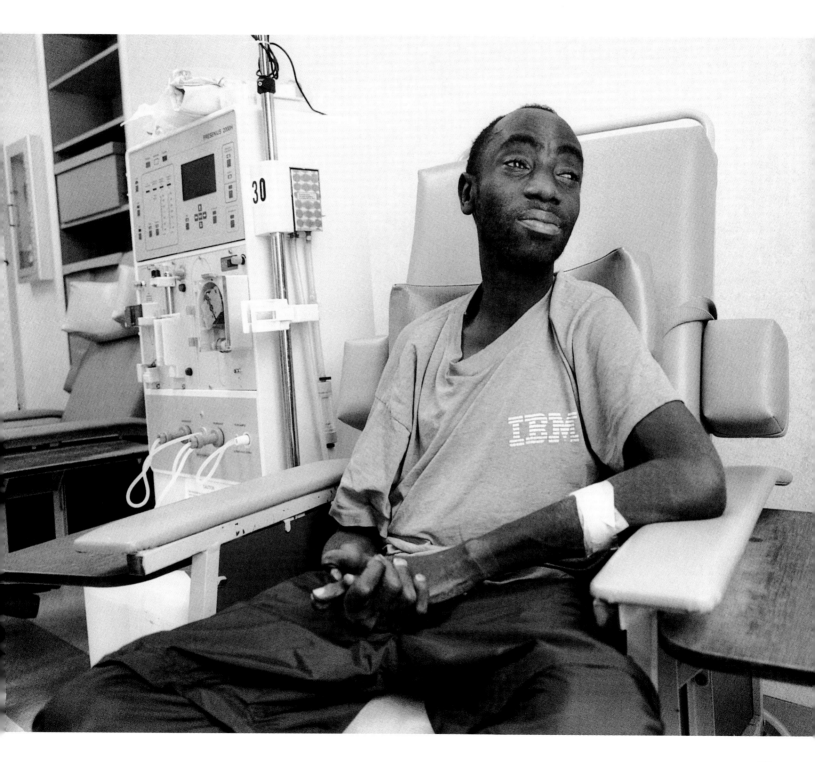

What does it mean to be an American? Ooooh! Goodness. I wouldn't think about being anything else! Heh heh. No, I just like America, for many reasons, I guess. Lots of reasons that you wish didn't exist but they do.

Fight for yourself. For what you think is right.
You're better off in the long run.

lois lane

Madison, Wisconsin
89 years old

The phone number listed for Lois Lane turned out to be outdated, and the people who currently have her old number got quite a kick out of my calling for "Lois Lane." Just another glimpse into what these folks go through every day.

Anyway, I located her at her new apartment in a retirement center in downtown Madison. Barely five feet tall, she's sharp as a tack, sprightly and good-humored, and has a sweet, almost huggable laugh. We talked for hours about her life's experiences in Montana, North Dakota, and mostly Wisconsin, as well as her travels around the world with the University of Wisconsin's alumni association tours.

Lois was interested in hearing about the other people I'd interviewed. She told me about a woman she knew who was 104 years old and had a beautiful outlook on everything, adding, "If I could live that long and be as bright and alert as she is, that would probably be the best dream I could have."

My mother and father separated when I was just a baby, so I never knew my father. They were young. And probably not ready for marriage. Who knows? It was right after that, my grandmother and uncle had this opportunity where you could squat on a piece of land out in Montana. Well, they made arrangements for my mother to come too with the babies. We lived out on the prairies of Montana for the first six years of my life.

I sure remember five of us living in that one-room shack on top of a hill. No water, no electricity, no anything. Twelve miles out of a little town called Guilford. We used to order groceries through the Sears Roebuck catalog. Can you imagine living there for six years? I guess I came from kind of rugged stock.

There probably weren't too many less fortunate growing up, but I never felt that way, because there was always a lot of love. The people around me just kind of laughed at life. They never seemed to get down. I don't know whether that's typical of the Irish. Kind of happy-go-lucky.

I've been in Madison since I got out of high school. I came to business college, and took a civil service examination and was with the state for over forty years, a secretary in the School of Pharmacy at the university for thirty. I never married. During the war years, it was buzzing with soldier boys. They'd go off. You'd keep in touch for a while. Someone would come back, and they'd want to pick up where they left off, and then by that time, you'd cooled off. Anyway, it was probably my fault in a lot of ways. Somebody wanted me and I wanted somebody else. You know how that goes.

And I guess I thought a lot about my mother, you know, the bad time it was for her. In those days, once you have been divorced from you husband, you can't get married again. It was too bad because she was a cute, lively little lady . . . young and fun . . . more like a sister than a mother. She was very close to me. I really missed her after she died. She worked so hard all her life. Just to keep us together.

No matter where I go, "Is that *really* your name?" I tell them, "Except I didn't have the nice shiny black hair." I first became aware of it when these little ole paperboys formed a club. They used to call me all the time. They wondered when Superman was coming, they wanted to meet him. The UPS man used to ring the doorbell and say, "The man of steel is here." That kind of stuff.

I've only lived here for less than a year. I needed to get someplace where if something happened to me—because I don't have family around. My sister is in Arizona and her daughter and children are all there. I don't travel anymore. And that's what I miss. They have a van here that takes you places. I sign up to go to the malls, grocery shopping, the bank, bookshops, or whatever. And then they always have entertainment. And all kinds of church services. I'm a putterer anyway. I'm sort of a news junkie, and PBS has good programs. I lost my vision pretty much. I just have a little part of my right eye that I can read with. And only with my magnifying glass. I can just sit and think sometimes. I spend a lot of time looking out the window.

I might have some regrets sometimes about not ever being married because you never have any children to care about you when get older. Probably not been so fussy. I don't know if I'd really call that a regret, just something you might be thinking about just sitting doing nothing. I'm proud of my heritage, content with what I've had. I guess I feel satisfied with what I have done with my life. Next year I will be in my nineties. ∎

If you want to get anywhere in the world, you have to do the work.

bruce lee

Amherst, Massachusetts
46 years old

I met Bruce, or Kimo, the middle name he also uses, at his house just a block and a half from the collegiate bustle of downtown Amherst. He gave me a tour of the home he shares with his wife, and their respective offices, and I even got to see a video on alpine snowboarding—my ignorance must have been apparent.

I was impressed by Bruce's earnest sense of exploration, manifest in the different places and lives he and his wife have lived, both apart and together. When we both got hungry, we crunched through the snow to Bertucci's for pizza, which is where I took this picture.

When we got back, Bruce's wife, Carrie, had returned from school, and I enjoyed talking with her as well before beginning the congested drive back into New York.

I was born in 1956, in Honolulu, Hawaii. My father was Chinese. My mother was Hawaiian and German. My sister and I grew up on the southeast part of Oahu, on the ocean coast. We had a little lagoon. During low tide I could walk around there and go crabbing. And then when the tide came in, you could fish or throw nets. I used to make boats out of corrugated roofing metal—U-shaped, like a canoe, with two-by-fours in the ends, covered with pitch. My father was really good with tools, and he showed me how to use them at a young age. I wanted to be an architect, but the school of architecture at the University of Hawaii was full, so I went into the fine arts. I eventually graduated with a degree in visual design.

I was in Hawaii up until I was twenty-eight, dating a woman from New York City. When we graduated, she wanted to come back to New York—arguably the mecca of graphic design. So I came back with her and started working. And I did that for eight years. The standard New York City thing . . . I had a couple of staff jobs with design firms, and then I got into freelancing. One cool thing was that I started surfing again on the Jersey shore. It tends to be such a rat race when you're just working. It was great to be out of the city, and be in the water and enjoy that again. Eventually I moved out to Hoboken and started dating another woman, who's now my wife.

We decided to move back to Hawaii for a couple of years. But there's not much staff work there in the advertising graphic design field. We had a group of friends that lived in the Berkshires—in a classic New England kind of a town, white church, peaked roofs. In '95, we came straight from Hawaii to the Berkshires. In the middle of November. The first place we lived in was a cabin that was wood-heated. So

one day I'm reading the newspaper on the beach near Waikiki—this is literal—and the next day I'm over here moving logs in to stoke the fire!

My wife decided she wanted to go back to school, so that's why we moved here. And it's really wonderful. The neighbors are really friendly; we socialize and hang out in the summer on the porches, you know. I never had that before. I work out of my house. What I do is I design and develop websites, mostly for businesses. I'm a former art director in advertising and before that, a graphic designer. I don't know how some people can stay in one career their whole lives. Mentally, you start to stagnate. The hard part of changing is there's usually a drop in income . . . but life is about growing. I'm studying for a master's in counseling psychology.

When men and women hit their forties, they start to reevaluate their lives. It's a point of examining your goals, letting go of unachieved ones, and making new ones and reassessing where you are. I think that's what I'm going through now. I get so many ideas, I could really fragment myself if I'm not careful, so I'm trying to say, well, do these two or three things, get those done, and then try the other things. Prioritize.

I believe that our thoughts create the reality around us. If I had to pigeonhole myself, I practice an Eastern philosophy. It's like Buddhism, but it's not . . . it's the *science* of the fire of the heart. In a basic sense, it's about developing a sense of living ethics. And a lot of it's meditation. Trying to live your life with joy in your heart. I think it results in a renewal that's ongoing. It's a big part of my life.

I've got a lot of good things going on, a lot of things to be happy about. There's pressure, a little financial stress; I don't know if that's unhappiness . . . I think a lot of life is the balance of things. ■

What does it mean to be an American? I think we're very fortunate to live here. Because we have a lot of the benefits and creature comforts, we live relatively safe lives. So to be a good American, I think we have a responsibility. To be aware of the good things that we have in our lives and to remember that the things that we do affect other people throughout the world—you know, our ideas and our technologies—and to act responsibly.

What does it mean to be an American? Oh! It means that we're the luckiest people in the world, and don't ever, ever take it for granted. Our forefathers and their forefathers sacrificed a lot of blood, sweat, and tears that we may be able to enjoy what we have today. "Not what your country can do for you, but what you can do for your country" is good words. I cannot say it enough. Thank you, Lord. It's the best thing in the world.

Sometimes, the harder you work, the luckier you get.

robert e. lee

Judith Gap, Montana
53 years old

I arrived early at the Lee Ranch, so I met Bob and Kathy Lee's car in the drive and we made our introductions as I helped carry groceries into the house. The three of us then sat around the dining room table talking over iced tea and cheese and crackers. Articulate and highly energetic, Bob seemed totally at ease answering questions and indeed directing conversation. To my delight, he proved equally comfortable in front of a camera when I photographed him a few mornings later at dawn as he began the day's work.

In describing life with Bob, Kathy said, "There's all sorts of those types of -aholics, and Bob is basically a workaholic. Some of his friends call him a PTO—a prime time operator."

Before I left, we jumped into the truck and Bob gave me a tour of the ranch. In the middle of a field, he suddenly cut the engine and whispered, "Look over there." A group of wild elk was grazing not thirty feet away. "Wait'll we tell Kathy what you got to see," he said.

I can't wait to get up in the mornings. Usually we start work at this time of the year at six-thirty in the morning . . . be it fencing, checking cows' water, repair work, moving cows, spraying weeds, whatever needs to be done. Whatever's the top priority that day. Right now, things are looking pretty good. We've had a pretty good shot of moisture. Last winter was tremendously open, which caused a little bit of stress on our alfalfa. But it was an excellent calving season. Usually we'll come in and have supper around six-thirty, seven, and then Kathy and I will go out and enjoy the out-of-doors. Have a look around, check cattle salt, water, whatever else. We spend a lot of time together, Kathy and I. We've been married thirty-two years and loved every minute of it. In agriculture, you have to be married to a spouse that understands. Otherwise it'd be an insurmountable task.

We're kind of a first-generation rancher. We took off on our own and it was pretty scary, but I'm so glad we did. You know, in this day and age, they say you can't start on your own. I think if you want something bad enough, you'll find a way to make it happen. But you've got to have a break or two, too.

We moved up here in '72, have three kids that are fetched up, raised up, whatever you want to call it, and kind of on their own. Kenny's back here on the ranch. The poor kids have never had a day off, but that's all right. Yeah, that's what makes family so special to us: working together, playing together, and praying together. Gives you a pretty broad base to stand on in this day and age.

I'm very fortunate to be raised in a strong Christian family. Sometimes in the ranching business, sometimes I think you need Him a little bit more. Not that all of us as humans don't need Him. But, boy, when things get tough around here, they get pretty tough. Mother Nature can be awful harsh.

I'm pretty proud of what we've done, what we've put together. We're definitely not the biggest, but we're definitely not the smallest either. We run a small grains operation, be it wheat and barley, and those are produced for sale, and then we have a cow-calf outfit. We have four hundred mama cows, and then we have the calves from them, and we send them to feed lots in the Midwest. It works good.

In 1997, this ranch was recognized as the National Environmental Stewardship Award winner for the nation. It was a very humbling experience, but it is something that we cherish and value highly. And through the Stewardship Award I do a lot of national work, talking about the good things ranchers do on their land.

With a name like Robert E. Lee, I think it naturally gives you an opportunity to live up to the name's worth of the great Southern general—such a gentleman and such a leader, a positive influence. He was the hope, the faith of the whole Southern armies . . . I've liked it. Shoot! It gives you an "in." People never forget you. You know, you never get a second chance to make that first impression.

I'd like to be known as a hard worker, a caring person to help other people. Innovative . . . 'Course, I'm a type A personality. I like to talk and visit and share ideas—not that we're trying to be better, but I'll share ideas. There's givers and takers in this world, and Kathy and I'd just as soon be givers. Oh my goodness, it's so much easier to be positive and put a smile on your face rather than moan and groan about everything. I love being a positive person. Probably I do talk too much. And probably it does make some people uncomfortable. But what the heck.

I found my peace and satisfaction in the out-of-doors. Working with my wife. You just can't buy those things. ■

I tell every student that I study Bible with: Don't listen to anybody. Do what you feel good about. That's the way you feel happy and successful. I believe in personal freedom.

abraham lincoln

Chicago, Illinois
43 years old

Pastor Abraham was one of my early interviews. I was charmed by his great American story as well as his enthusiasm, earnestness, and warmth. We'd been rushed for pictures and the few hasty ones we took came out poorly, so we agreed that next time I was in the area, we'd get together again to take his picture.

A couple years went by. Finally, one night, I decided to call. When I asked for Pastor Lincoln, there was a silence and then I was informed that there had been a fire at his home the night before. And he had died in the fire. I was so upset! I cried and ranted and decided to print up the pictures of him that I did have, to give to family and friends at his service. I was up all night doing this, and when I went to FedEx them the following day, I realized that if the house had burned down, I needed a new address. So I called the number I'd called the previous day and explained that I had pictures of Pastor Abraham I'd like to send for the service. Again, a silence on the other end of the receiver. Something seemed amiss. I said, "Well, Pastor Abraham died, didn't he?" And she said, "Noooooo, that was Pastor LEE!" Sad for the loss of their pastor, I was, nonetheless, relieved that Pastor Abraham was okay. He and I had a good laugh at my expense when we finally did meet up again.

Abraham was a Christian name that I picked up when I was in the university. So then when I came to America, I just added the Lincoln. That's how Abraham Lincoln came about.

I come from India. Nagaland. That part of India, we don't use family name. Just one name, just like Bible name. Isaac. Jacob. Longrichang. But being American is to have a real American name. Obviously, you know, Lincoln is a real American name. So that was one reason. Other than that, also there is the man, himself, his person. He was a great man in the sense that he was a very, very honest man and also a man of integrity, I think, and those are qualities that really I admire.

We had to change so much . . . Driver's license, social security, and then her work place and then her name card and everything. And we had to go down to the court, twice. And . . . wow! She was very, very patient with me in all this.

My wife is a simple woman. A lot of people think that she is a nurse because she is so young. She became a doctor when she was twenty-five and now she's thirty-five. She would say, my husband is a minister. She is very proud of that. She thinks of me as a very important person. We've got four kids.

My goal is—again coming back to being an American—I believe that God wants to use America as a city on a hill. To be an instrument of righteousness, if we use the Bible language, as a kingdom of priests in a holy mission. I feel that America can do it. And God made America that way.

American Baptist missionaries were the ones who came to my part of India. I mentioned that my grandfathers were headhunters, you know. Oh, we didn't talk about that? Yeah, the American Baptist missionaries were the ones that first came to evangelize that area. Our people were at

that time really, the term is, uh, savage, you know, and headhunters. So, the miracle is, I don't know how it happened, everybody became Christian and my grandfather was the first one to be converted. For me, coming here, America, is just a way to say, "Thank you, Americans, for leading us to the gospel light." I think cross-cultural evangelism is pretty new in an American context.

I'm not yet a citizen, but I'm just waiting for the interview. If you become an American citizen, at that time you can change your name too. I will have no problem with that! I should have done that long ago but, for some reason, I just delayed. But I don't feel that just because I don't have a citizenship . . . actually in real life, I feel that I am an American. To me—this is kind of funny but—the way you *think* makes you American. Does that make sense?

One of the biggest challenges, I think always, is to overcome the culture. You know a little bit how India is, kinda slow pace—nothing about good or bad—but here, life is so fast. I've been here ten years but still, it's a challenge for me. To cultivate that kind of a highly sophisticated way of thinking is a big challenge. I do not know when I can overcome that. But . . . I'm trying. Honestly, one of my constant worries is how my kids are going to grow in this fast, you know, very sophisticated society. You go to school and the kids pull out their gun and bang, bang, bang, bang, bang. God! That makes me worried what we are becoming. But I guess I learned to trust God for my life and for my children's future.

I'm optimistic. And in fact that's a secret that may keep me going. Never give up. Yeah, persistence. In whatever you do. There's nothing you cannot do. You know, there's nothing you cannot overcome. I think if I have an advice, it would be, don't give up. That's my own advice to me. ■

What does it mean to be an American? **All the immigrants, down through all these years, came here to look for freedom. That's what makes a mind American. That's very, very unique. Because not many societies have that kind of binding factor. Americans are different in the sense that they really have a heart for other people. That Americans have the ability to give, the ability to serve others around the world.**

What does it mean to be an American? The most important thing is our freedom. We're very fortunate to be able to participate in the political system the way we can—there's just not enough people take an interest. I want to see women be
treated like equals, not just lip service. I've always worked for women, and I'd like to see more of them in public office. I
have two sons that served in the military. To protect our country. I've always been very proud of that.

Who am I? I'm a mother. I'm a grandmother. I'm a professional woman. I come from a working-class family. I've always worked hard. I've always lived by the golden rule.

marilyn monroe

Des Moines, Iowa
62 years old

After a brush with a mountain lion in Ohio Pyle State Park two nights before the interview, I decided to scrap the beauty of hike-in camping for a better night's sleep in an R.V. campground literally alongside the highway, not far from the Monroes' apartment on the outskirts of Des Moines.

Organized and affable, Marilyn had prepared several pages of notes, addressing questions outlined in my introductory letter and detailing stories related to her name that she thought might be of particular interest to readers. She chatted easily, while Bill Monroe, her second husband, offered wry commentary from time to time.

I walked away with a "Marilyn Monroe for Secretary of State" campaign poster and the feeling that they were rooting for me.

I was born right here, during the Depression, about two blocks from the capitol. So when I got into politics my father always said, "Well, I know you'll go far, you'll go to Des Moines," and I said, "Why, Papa?" and he said, "Because you were born in the shadow of the dome."

I had three children before I was twenty-one. I got married very young, right out of high school. Raising three little boys, we just couldn't make it on just one salary, so I went to work at Champion's Sparkplugs, which was the big plant in Burlington, Iowa. I got very active in the union. It was my job to represent our local at political events and to educate our membership. It wasn't too long after that that International UAW smiled upon me and I was taken out on staff. I went around the state of Iowa and helped organize Democratic headquarters.

In 1970, the incumbent at the County Recorder's Office retired and everyone said, "Marilyn, you know everyone in Des Moines County, you've knocked on every door, why don't you run?" The union was then talking about getting women more involved, so I went to the head honcho—the man to see in the state of Iowa if you were in the International UAW—and said, "You've always talked about me eventually becoming the upper echelon of the International UAW. How far do you think I am from it?" And he said, "Oh, probably about ten years . . . though it sure has never happened." "Well," I said, "knowing that, I'm going to venture out on my own." So that's what I did. I served for sixteen years as the County Recorder.

I worked hard and the voters continued to elect me. I had some tough elections, but I knew politics and I knew organization. The day I walked in to take office, I said to the staff, "You and I are going to work together. I'm going to be here for four years, and if you don't want to work with me, I guess you won't be here." Most of that staff is still there today.

When I was on the campaign trail, I loved to introduce myself as Marilyn Monroe. I always used to tell them, "Remember, she was Norma Jean Baker—I'm the real Marilyn Monroe." So that was kind of my opening line. As soon as they see your name, they have to make a comment: "Are you a blonde?" I'd say, "No, I'm a strawberry blonde." "How's Joe or Jack?" I'd say, "I haven't seen him recently." "Can you sing?" "Well, the best I can do is Happy Birthday.'" And everybody'd laugh and it was always okay.

One time we went to check in at the airport in Nashville and: "Oh my God, Bill Monroe in Nashville, Tennessee—the King of the Bluegrass!'" And then he looked at mine: "Marilyn Monroe! I can't believe it, the two of you together. There's no way you're going to leave Nashville other than in first class." And I'd never flown first class in my life.

Our life has changed a lot. I retired in January after twenty-seven years of public service. I was going to continue on until sixty-five but my husband fell ill. Now both of us read a lot. I cook. We sold our sports cars and we bought us a van. We've traveled 13,000 miles in our van, basically to see family. Together we have seventeen grandchildren. I have to go to a discount card store for birthday cards!

My biggest concern right now is the quality of life that my husband and I are having after working all these many years. Because you work for retirement to enjoy life. There are so many things that I want to do yet that I haven't done.

I think my greatest accomplishment is my three sons. I really do. I feel like coming from a working-class family and being able to serve the public, both county and state, was a good accomplishment. Especially being a working mother. ∎

> Just go out and do it. You're going to make mistakes and stuff, but unless you make mistakes, you aren't trying.

richard nixon

Boise, Idaho
52 years old

Supposedly some of my ancestors came over on the Mayflower. A relative fought in the War of 1812. I also have relatives that fought in the Revolutionary War. And if we had paid annual dues, my son would be a S.A.R. and my daughter would be a D.A.R. I think my aunt is still a member. In fact, my grandfather on my mom's side ran the last paddle wheel boat on Lake George. Western New York is really deep in historical type stuff because it was one of the thirteen colonies and everything. It's a lot different than it is out here, historical-wise.

I grew up south of Buffalo on a dairy farm. The town was only 1300 people. Most of my family's still there. There were five kids, all within five years of each other's age. Our mother died when we were young. It was kind of difficult, but the five of us were so close. My dad remarried and had five more.

One of my brothers is my mirror twin—identical, but I'm left-handed and he's right-handed. He's back east and we're still pretty close. His name's Edward. Richard Nixon had a brother named Edward too. Even though we weren't named after him. It just happened that way.

I get all kinds of responses. People ask if I'm related and I say, "Yeah, he's my uncle." Then they all try to figure out what they should say: "Well, he wasn't *that* bad, he just got caught . . ." And then there's always the people that say, "Yeah, and I'm Spiro Agnew."

I was in junior high when he lost to Kennedy. Every time I got on the bus: "Nixon's a loser!" When I was in the Air Force, the *Air Force Times* did an article on the front page: *Top of the Line and Bottom of the Line: Nixon at the Top, Nixon at the Bottom.* Also, a guy in our barracks invited me to be a groomsman in his wedding.

One of the other groomsmen, his name was Ronald Reagan. No relation. The paper in Oklahoma City did an article: *Richard Nixon and Ronald Reagan, Groomsmen in Local Wedding.* It's always been sort of fun. Easy name to remember.

I socialize and play golf. I don't have time for a lot of hobbies. I think of myself as a workaholic. I mean every job I've had, it's been ten-, twelve-hour days. Whatever the job takes. I used to be one of the techies. I was in it so deep, I had screens on three different systems and I used to sit there and work on all three of 'em and talk on the phone at the same time. I thought about changing professions . . . Sales rep! I'm kind of a people person anyway. I don't know, can you change professions in your fifties?

My wife is a native Boisian, and you don't move Boisians. I mean, if you spend any time here . . . our winters are real mild—maybe there was three weeks we didn't play golf last winter. Summers, humidity is only 20 or 25 percent. We go on vacation back to the east usually for two weeks, and after a week we look at each other and say, "Can't take this." Boise per capita has the most number of millionaires anymore. And quite a number of world headquarters. But Boise is a real small community. Yeah, I know an awful lot of people in town because I served in the Air Force and have been in business for so many years.

I'm outgoing enough that people yell out, "Hello, Mr. Nixon!" And it still embarrasses my wife . . . She refuses to vote with me because after we vote, they announce your name. When they say, "Richard Nixon has voted," everyone stops voting and stares. We've had a lot of fun over the years. ∎

Richard Nixon struck me as having a healthy sense of irreverence. He laughs a lot, and it's an intense, inside-joke sort of laugh. I enjoyed taking his picture especially, because he is extremely expressive.

Inspired by his talk of Boise, I spent the next morning ambling around its charming downtown before heading north through this incredibly beautiful state.

What does it mean to be an American? My generation worked hard to get where we are. Things weren't just handed to us like they are to kids nowadays. Plus, immigration has been way out of whack for too long. I'm still confused why the U.S. should be the haven for every destitute people in the world. We aren't even feeding our own poor. Yet still, the United States is the greatest country in the world. I mean, when they play the national anthem, I get teary-eyed.

> Age only tells you how long you've been on the planet. But other than that, it's a state of mind.

scarlett o'hara

Swoyersville, Pennsylvania
46 years old

When I first reached Scarlett by phone, I learned in her excellent, tobacco-cured voice that she's a Territory Sales Manager at Philip Morris, rides a Harley, and is into heavy metal. Perfect! She sounded sharp and fun and full of piss and spit. And so she is. We had a good ol' time hanging out on her patio on one of the last warm evenings of the fall in peaceful Swoyersville. And she made trips to the garage beer meister to replenish our beverages. Her husband, Bob Lee, joined us after a long day of dealing with an unruly tenant in one of the many properties they own and manage. It was Saturday night, so we headed to their favorite bar for wings, fries, and more hanging out.

Scarlett's close to her family and spoke often and warmly of them.

Bob said of Scarlett, "She's an honest woman who's as much man as she is woman. And not afraid to let you know. She'll never let you down, never stand you up, but she'll tell you where the bear shits in the woods."

I bought a bike when I was thirty. A 450 Suzuki. All's I was ever doing on the bike was making big ovals. I didn't understand the concept of leaning. I'm trying to turn the handlebars. Bad thing to do. I said, that's it. I'm gonna take the course.

As soon as I pulled into the place—it was at the YMCA—I saw this guy standing outside. Big tall guy, long hair, smoking a cigarette, he had a gray shirt on, black suspenders, black pants, black boots, and glasses that were tinted. You know a lot of the people that go to the Y are very preppy, with their yellow plaid shorts and their little polo shirts and their sweaters tied around their neck. He was the only one I seen in color, you know what I mean? And he was really in black and white.

I got into the classroom and there he is. I figured he was a biker, but he happened to be one of the instructors. They said, "This is Bob. He's up here from Swoyersville." And I thought to myself, "Where the *hell* is Swoyersville?" Little did I ever think I'd be living in Swoyersville. I was in Scranton at the time. I've been here six years.

It was a two-week class . . . Two nights of classroom and then four nights of range, and one of those range nights was your test. I said, I'm getting my license on my own merits, and once I have my license and I've passed this course, I'm having that man.

After Bob and I started dating I had a 450 Honda rebel for a couple years. I've been able to change the plugs and clean 'em and stuff like that. But uh, I'm not going to pretend to be a mechanic, I don't want to break down on the side of the road—triple A! A little secret, I've never had to change a tire either, shhhhhh!

I went from a 450 Honda to a 1340 Harley, 1980, strip down dresser, shovel head. You get such attitude when you get off of it. And then you go to a party and when you show up on the bike you just survey the crowd and look around and it's like, "I'm here."

It's a lot of fun. Bikers are great people. It's not that my husband and I are die-hard. The bikes sometimes sit in the garage for months because we get busy with other projects, but we love riding and we love getting together with other people that enjoy the sport as well. And as I've gotten older, we have more friends come to our home. Like you used to be younger and hang out at the bar with your friends. I like to drink my beer. Now I hang out here and I go to my beer meister. It's a lot cheaper. And I got the frosted mugs . . . no extra charge. I like socializing, hanging out, smoking ciggies, drinkin' beer and bullshittin.' I'm a little rough around the edges—my mother would say I got this steel coating with nothing more than a marshmallow center.

We purchased twenty-five acres of wooded land in a place called Belmont. It's a half hour from here. We're camping now. We have the Simpson Street Party Bus parked up there. About five of our family and friends have permanent sites with tents. And they all have their fire rings and we have a lovely time. And eventually, yeah, we'll have a house up there.

I was born Scarlett O'Hara. Catholic church was not happy about it, though. So my parents said, Okay, we'll put Elizabeth on there. I've never been called it in my life. On my driver's license it says E. Scarlett O'Hara, and people say, What's the E stand for? I say, Excellent. ∎

What does it mean to be an American? **The bottom line is that we're all proud that our ancestors—whether it be your immediate parents, your grandparents, your great grandparents, or whatever—that they came to this country and thank the good Lord that they did. You may have been born here, but you wouldn't have been if your ancestors didn't come from somewhere else and settle here.**

It'll give me peace of mind to know I brought 'em up right.
To do the right things.

rosa parks

Durham, North Carolina
35 years old

With Rosa's busy schedule, I had to call at all odd hours of the day to even catch her, and I'd begun to doubt her existence. But she generously agreed to meet me on her "day off"—a day she was working only one of her jobs. We sat in her kitchen one warm North Carolina spring afternoon, while her mother watched soaps on the fifty-two-inch TV Rosa had bought her for Christmas. Her son, daughters, and twin brother (they were the youngest of thirteen) all passed through at one point or another.

Clearly disciplined and determined, Rosa also has a great sense of humor and an infectious laugh, which I tried to catch on film as we joked about our first cars—hers an old Nova and mine mostly Toyota.

A big Carolina fan, she says people ask her why she works for Duke but doesn't pull for Duke. She tells them, "I cheer for 'em. Every time they give me my check, I cheer for them."

When I was born, my mom let a nurse name me. Rosa. And it so happened my dad's last name was Parks. I get letters, I get phone calls: they said, "Ohhhhh, you're the Rosa Parks that wouldn't go to the back of the bus?" "Are you *the* Rosa Parks?" "No, I'm not," I said. "I would like to be."

I was born in Durham, all my life in Durham. I had nine brothers—yes, nine brothers—and three sisters. So in all, it was thirteen kids. I'm the youngest, me and my twin brother, we're the babies. We're like night and day. He's like night and I'm like day!

I get up, make sure my kids get off to school, and then I go to work. I've been working at Duke in environmental services for sixteen years. Mainly what I do is just doctors' sleep rooms. Like doctors that stay overnight or on call. I don't get off until six-thirty. I just come home enough to get my smock. I have to be at Wal-Mart at seven-thirty. About six months now, I been working at Wal-Mart, part-time. As a cashier. Because I have bills I'm trying to pay off quick and save a little money. I get off at twelve. Midnight.

My oldest daughter, she'll be nineteen, June the thirtieth. I was very young when I had her. I was in my sophomore year. It was very hard because I was young, I didn't really know anything about kids, you know I got caught and it was a mistake. But my mom told me that she would stand by me. My mom and my dad told me I wasn't going to drop out, so, you know, while I was going to school they used to take care of her for me.

It was very difficult, going to school, coming home, taking care of her, making sure she was fed and a bath and everything. Sometimes I had to wait till she go to sleep before I could do my homework. Couldn't really go nowhere unless I take her with me . . . Everything got cut off. After I had my daughter, I knew I had to get out and get a job. But my biggest dream is, if I can one day, to go to college to be an R.N.

I try not to tell her that she was a mistake. I just tell her, I'm not saying that it was a mistake, but on my part, I didn't listen to my mom, and I tell them I would like for them to listen to me. Because the road that I traveled, I don't want them to travel down. I want them to finish school—I finished school—but I also want them to go to college. And if they decide that, you know, down the road, that they want to have kids or whatever, they won't have to work so hard to take care of them. Because times are very hard now—it's harder than when I was growing up—so I try to give them advice to stay in school, to graduate and go to college. And, you know, make something better of themselves.

I'm proud of my daughter. She works, she has chorus practice, plus she goes to school. She's getting ready to graduate in May and she's going to college. She want to be an R.N. too. So I stand behind her one hundred percent. And Duke's gonna help. They going to pay like 80 percent and I got to pay 20 percent. And I'm trying to get her some grants and stuff, too.

My son, he'll be sixteen, he is a trip: "Mom, c'mon, let me driiive." He's working and trying to save him some money up to help get him a car. I told him, I said, "Your first might not look like you want it, but you can always save up and get you another one later on down the line." And my baby, she's just turned thirteen. Yeah, and no more. My baby, she's about old enough to take care of herself, but I really don't like leaving her on my mom . . .

Mainly I worry about my kids . . . how they

What does it mean to be an American? To me, it means, we get our *freedom*. We have the freedom to go anywhere that we want to go.

feel about not spending enough time with me. And I try to keep them under control and still try to work. If they ask me can they do something and if I don't think it's right, I'm not going to let them do it. So they might tell their friends that, "My mom is mean." Like my oldest daughter, she'd say, "My mom is mean, but I still love my mom, but she's kind of a little on the strict side." My son, he'd say I was just *mean*.

I be telling him, "If I don't feel that it's right, I'm not going to let you do it. You know, you gonna to call me *mean*, you gonna say I'm hateful or whatever, whatever, but if I feel like you're hanging around the wrong crowd, I'm not going to let you join that crowd. Because I really care about you. I care about what happens to you, and this world is so wicked."

Whenever they go off to college it will be sad, but I'll think, you know, it'll give me some peace of mind. As long as they call me every now and then. Or I might just go up there to see them. They'll be like, "Momma, why you ain't tell me you was coming?!"

I'm proud of my kids. I'm proud of my mom, she helps out a lot. I'm proud of myself. I'm working two jobs and still kind of being there for them. I try to explain to my friends, "I have a lot of stuff on my mind that I'm trying to achieve right now with my kids. So if I just go get quiet, go to my own little world, you know, just let me, and I'll be all right." ■

What does it mean to be an American? Well, that you got your freedom so far, and we're fightin' to keep it every day, hon. And we'll continue to fight until, you know, we make sure we have it every day.

If you tell somebody you're going to do something, you're going to do it. Because your word's worth all there is in this world.

edgar allen poe

Comanche, Oklahoma
47 years old

For one technical reason or another, a few of my interviews had to be redone, and Edgar Allen Poe's was one of them. But it was a wonderful excuse to get back to Comanche to see both Ed and Connie Poe again. This time I arrived early and had dinner with Connie; Ed was on the night shift at the water plant. Once we'd caught up and finished dinner, we hopped in her van and drove the few miles to the plant where we sat down and talked with Ed, who was in fine form and full of jokes.

Between spending time with his grandsons, shuttling his mother back and forth to the doctors, and helping various relatives with outside projects, Ed clearly makes family a big part of his life, and vice versa. As Poe put it, "I do the honey do's for everybody, so they think I'm just about it."

They promised we'd hit the slots up the road the next time I visited.

There was a show that come on TV back in the days, it's called *The Name Is the Same*. And my mother and them named me Edgar Allen Poe—hoping they'd get on this show, win money. But we didn't get that far. I just got the name.

I have a lot of fun with it. You say "Edgar Poe," and: "Your middle name wouldn't be Allen?" And I say, "Oh, yeah." And they think it's real cute, and it is. To have that recognition. I broke my leg one time, and this old gal in the emergency room, she said my name, and I walked up there and I said, "Did you call me?" "No, some idiot signed Edgar Allen Poe." And I said, "Well, I'm the idiot."

I thought about naming my son after me and my wife really didn't want to. Thought it would be too much on him. So I was gonna name him Fishing. Fishing Poe. That or Electric.

We've been married for twenty-eight years as of last month. I put up with her for that long I haven't got time for any of the other ones . . . when she turned forty, I was gonna swap her in for two twenties (well, I got to spice this book up!). Got two kids. I got three grandkids and no great grandkids yet.

I play guitar. We got this little old band together and we was playing at nursing homes and things like that. I enjoy it. I've done a lot of Elvis Presley stuff. They had a telethon, Jerry Lewis telethon and I got on there—a gal made me an Elvis suit—and I got on there and did some stuff for that. My daughter was singing with us some. It just don't seem like we get together like we used to.

My daughter, she's got a voice on her like you wouldn't believe. I took her to Star Search in Oklahoma City. She really got cheated on that . . . they switched judges right in the middle, so how could you justify that? 'Course it upset *her*. She's kind of like me, when you get over that last little ol' hump, but somebody's always beating her.

I'd just have to say I'm a Baptist, I guess, I like fried chicken and all that stuff . . . Politics? I'm just smart enough to stay out 'em, hon, that's all I can tell you. I just stay away from it. I'm a Democrat—my grandmother said there wasn't no way she raised a Republican.

I run this water plant. Make sure the water's good to drink and stuff, make sure they've got plenty of water to last them all night so that the next morning they're not out of water. First went to work for the city of Comanche in '81 and I've been with them ever since. This particular job, I've been out here probably about ten years. Hope I get to retire from here. Probably another fifteen before I can do that. Usually I work three days through the day and then two nights, nights. If the night man take off I've got to work his shifts. I used to work all nights.

I worry about everything. Bills, health, and everything I guess. There's a war going on, you worry about what's going to happen to this whole country. And the crap that's going on that shouldn't be. Like the Twin Towers in New York. That's a shame.

You know I've been blessed. I've got a good family and we've got us three grandchildren. I got my mother still here, and I got a grandmother, ninety-seven years old. She may be here till she's a hundred. Smarter than you and I both! I'm thankful for everything. The food we've got on our table. And, you know, having the freedom.

I ain't had too many complaints about me. ■

I put God first in everything I do.

elvis presley

Houston, Texas
42 years old

I drove into Houston on one of its distinctly hot and sticky days. Elvis Presley and I met at a local wings joint he'd suggested, grabbed a glass of iced tea, and began our conversation over the music and substantial general din. Straightforward and relaxed, Elvis smiled easily and genuinely.

After going through the questions, Elvis took me to the baseball field where he coaches Little League and then his home in a quiet, shady neighborhood where we shot this picture with his kids in their minivan. It is a favorite of mine.

If I'm introduced to somebody, you know, they say, "Oh, by the way, this is Elvis," not, "This is Elvis Presley." I just want to be normal like everyone else. "Hey, you got your blue suede shoes?" or "Can you sing 'Jailhouse Rock'?" Everybody gets about one or two shots and that's it.

Would I have chosen it? Doesn't matter. I've had it for so long, it's grown on me . . . The story I was told was that my father's best friend, they made an agreement that when they got married, they would name each firstborn son after each other. When I came along he made good on his promise. His friend's name was Elvis Christopher.

I'm a true Texan, bred and fed. From Dallas. Married, three kids—five in all: two from a previous marriage. The ones at home are seven, nine, and eleven. The other two are fourteen and twenty-one. I'm a data center supervisor at Memorial Herman, a hospital, just down the street. Been with them about ten years. I've only been on the day shift, seven to three-thirty, for about two years. Before that, I was graveyard, eleven at night to seven-thirty in the morning. I mean, that has its advantages to it. When the kids were smaller, they pretty much never went to day care. My wife works for the post office.

Things aren't really the same as when I was coming up, kids getting on computers, getting on the Internet, you know, Sega, Nintendo. The biggest thing I had to play with coming up was the corner pinball machine. It's just so much opportunity out there for them now. The biggest challenge for the kids' generation is staying on track. It's almost like you have too many things to choose from. Not to mention the drugs, and peer pressure—and I know it's coming . . . I'm trying to lay a little foundation now.

I do some Little League and football coaching—my son's on the team. My girl's cheerleading. And then my girls are in Brownies and Scouting. Yeah, from one ride to the next: Little League, football, Girl Scouts, Brownies, other than that, pretty much church. A movie once every blue moon.

You know, I look back and see some of the mistakes that I made, and if I had the chance to do them over I probably would, I probably would have stayed in college and got to my master's program, just gone straight through as opposed to coming out and saying, "I want to make money." You know, I finished college about three years later than I should have.

When I dropped out I was driving a truck, and I just looked into the crystal ball and said, "Do I want to look back twenty years from now and say I went three quarters of the way through college?" And I started doing a bunch of hypotheses and what-ifs. "What if I would have finished school?" I just couldn't see myself being a fifty-year-old truck driver—not that there's anything wrong with it, but I knew that that's not how I wanted to end up.

I've always pretty much been an independent person, always wanted to own my own business. It's not too late. I've had a couple ideas that I let get away from me, a couple of opportunities also. Right now, if I could do anything, I would open up some family entertaining thing, maybe like a bowling and batting cage, or some kind of odd combination thing. I probably will try it eventually. I'd like to see it happen.

I'm a big kidder and joker. I just like having fun. It's not that I don't take things serious, but I try not to dwell on things I can't really control or stop from happening. I take it the way it is and move right through it. My kids would probably say, He's a good father, and my wife would probably say, He's a good husband. And I think my friends would say I'm easy to get along with. I don't pull any punches. ■

What does it mean to be an American? Maybe at one time in our history, you know, as a black American, maybe one time in our history we weren't allowed certain opportunities. And to some extent now it's even still true. But on the broader picture, there are opportunities out there. There's no excuse for you not to have any type of education, any type of skills. Because there are zillions of government-funded programs where you can get the training, but it's up to you. It's your choice. So if you choose not to do it, you choose to live like you want to live. That's the one thing that ties us all together: the freedom to do what you want, religion, whatever. It goes back to the Constitution. It's there for you, but it's up to you to move on it.

Quit beating yourself up and just realize that you are a good person. Attitude is everything—it's up to you to determine how you're going to respond to things.

ronald reagan

Spokane, Washington
39 years old

"Well," Ron said once we'd sat down to talk in his suburban Spokane home, "if you want excitement, you definitely picked the wrong person." But his stories and sound advice on meeting life's adversity—most poignantly with respect to parenting his children—have arisen in my mind time and again since we've met, at twists and turns I've encountered on my own road. Ron's definitely not afraid to call a spade a spade and admits he's been told he's too honest.

I laughed to reread in the interview Ron's July 2000 prognostication, when notions of a rosy new economic order were far more de rigueur: "The economy scares the heck out of me. It's been too good for too long. We're due. I don't care if that's a pessimistic view or not, we're due." Shoulda listened.

I come from an interesting family . . . I was born in Lewiston, Idaho. My mom married my father when she was an eighth grader and quit school. They were married and in the army—Alaska first, then Fort Rucker, Alabama. We spent five years there, but in that time, my mom left my father. So he had custody of us I want to say a year, maybe two. And all of a sudden, he had to go to the Korean War. So, packed us up, made the cross-country trip, and dropped us off on Mom's front doorstep. Haven't seen him since. Nah, actually one other time, four, five years later, he picked us up in the afternoon type thing.

She ended up remarrying and we moved to Pierce, Idaho, a small logging community. To be honest, before my mom married my dad, we were all hellraisers. My mom was working nights. She'd come home and go to bed. We were raising ourselves there for a while . . . We did just about everything we could to get in trouble.

Our stepdad instilled discipline and responsibility. We all know what it is to toe the line . . . and we all have better relationships with him now than we had when we were at home.

I was kind of a workaholic and my whole goal was to be promoted—and I think that's *why* I got divorced the first time. I don't care about the corporate ladder anymore, I want to be closer to my kids so I have more chances to be a part of their life. I've got to make my wife happy, I've got to make my kids happy, I've got to make myself happy.

I'm in a blended family now. I have two kids that come every other weekend, and my wife's children of course. I would say probably 89 percent of our arguments are over the kids, so blending things, it's hard. No kids between us; I said, two eight-year-olds, a ten- and an eleven-year-old, that's plenty.

The biggest thing I worry about is how the kids are gonna turn out. I mean, coming from broken families, you know. To get through high school, college, and be somewhat stable in their lives, but yet have a good time. I don't care if my kid's a valedictorian, I don't care if my kid's the star basketball player, what I care is that whatever they do, they try with all their heart. I want 'em to be responsible and have discipline the way I did. But less than I did. I want them to relax more than me.

With the job I have now, I go see doctors and I try to convince them why my drugs are better than the competition's drugs and try to get their commitment to prescribe that drug. I took the job recently to be closer to my children. I'm usually out of town three nights a week. So I spend a lot of time in hotel rooms.

For a while, you know, I'd show up from out of town to do business and there'd be no place for me to stay. Even now I'll say at the end of the conversation, "Now, this is no joke. This is Ronald Reagan, or Ron Reagan, and I will be there."

I've always had a dream of owning my own business, but I've never—to be quite honest—had the guts to do it. When it gets right down to the nitty gritty, I grab for security. Overall, I'm proud of where I'm at in life today. I've made good and bad decisions, and yeah, it saddens me I've got a divorce on my record. But at that same time, I love my wife. I love her kids. I love my kids and to my knowledge we're happy.

When I was kid, my hero was Reggie Jackson. Because he was Mr. Clutch, he always came through. Well, without sounding, you know, like a religious fanatic, God is my hero; I mean, I try to do the right things every day. ∎

What does it mean to be an American? Even when we think things are bad, they're not bad. The most amazing thing is to listen to people gripe about how tough they have it . . . We're fortunate. I count my lucky stars that I live here and not someplace else.

Tomorrow they'll understand. Today I'm a fool.

paul revere

Embassy of Heaven,
Stayton, Oregon
12 years reborn

In my search for a Paul Revere, I came across the Embassy of Heaven Web site, which declared: "It is the Eleventh Hour! Pastor Paul Revere is on a midnight ride urging you to awake . . . for now is our Salvation . . ." I decided to get in touch.

When I explained the project to Pastor Paul over the phone, he said, "I don't think I can participate in your project because I don't consider myself a citizen of the United States." "Oh?" "I'm a citizen of Heaven." I explained that that didn't matter, my interest was capturing life across the country. So he told me a bit of his story—how the Oregon National Guard had removed them from their land—but assured me that they were peace-loving people and that he was happy to talk to anyone to get the word out. So we arranged a meeting.

When I pulled up to the gate in rural Oregon, Pastor Paul was waiting to unlock the gate for me and relock it back behind us. Having done so, he sped off into the property in his car as I followed quickly in mine.

When you came into the place, there was a great big sign that said: Entering Heaven.

We worked the thirty-four acres—it was a beautiful, gorgeous place. We groomed it—I mean, when people'd come in, I'd put 'em to work. We had a huge picnic area up on top, a bonfire place, an open-door kitchen area where people would come, wood stoves and also propane, and over to the east we had a gravity-fed shower system, a building with a glass door, skylights, a printing press room, there were computer stations, we had a baptismal hole . . . We were getting ready to build a chapel, a two-story chapel, when they took us out—we got the foundation in but that was it . . . We had wonderful things there. We were there for twenty years making our investment of life into the place, our expression of love and Christianity.

It was not an eviction. It was what they called an ejection, yeah—January thirty-first, 1997. There was no court, no hearings, no positions in law. It was a hundred percent military operation. They brought in, basically, their army. And the Oregon National Guard. They were brought in on a wineries tour bus. Well, it was a military operation under disguise. Except for the tanks, the tanks were obvious. They had people from different jurisdictions, county, city, SWAT teams, federal, state, I mean, you name it and they were there. So they came in with their war machines, tanks, machine guns—though we had nothing. We had one .22 rifle. It was there because, you know, we're out in the country.

I mean, we stood up. We voiced our objection. In fact, the first words out of my mouth were, "In the name of Jesus Christ, remove yourself from God's sanctuary." They immediately took me into custody with no cause. There was no

warrants for my arrest, there was nothing, they took me directly into custody. They claim they charged me with interfering with governmental process. It was a fraudulent charge, it was a malicious charge. They took all the men; they were gonna take everybody. Children were going to go to Children's Services, the women, the men all were going to go to jail, that's what the plans were. Well, there's a few events that took place that fouled things up, so Rachel was released, the children, and oh, mental retards. The mental guy that we were taking care of and had been for a year, they didn't know how to deal with him. So they finally threw the women and the children and the mental retard out on the street, and took all the men to jail.

If you'd been there on January thirty-first, if you'd been on the Embassy grounds, very good chance you would have gone to jail. You got to remember, there were no warnings. No signs, no postings, no services, no acts of law. The papers required for an eviction or for—they call it ejection, for a tax foreclosure—there was nothing met according to their own system of law.

Technically, according to the United States law, they are not allowed to do military operations on American soil. Unless they have declared war. Well, the way they got around it is there is a declared war on drugs, so they can use military operations on drug wars. Well, there was no drug war here. The tanks were justified for hostage recovery—as if we had stolen somebody. That's pretty flimsy. It's been since found that none of us were guilty of interfering with governmental process.

When they went in, they smashed the offering box and stole all the funds of the church, for what they claimed in tax. These were donations to God's purpose, it was not theirs to take. Why did

97

I admit to some misgivings: I nearly choked when he made a Jimmy Jones joke as I politely sipped the iced tea his wife, Rachel, had graciously served. My initial suspicions, however, proved as ludicrous as theirs—that I was FBI. We spent hours talking together on one of the gutted school buses that became home and ministry once their compound was seized. As with so many pastors, Pastor Paul is as articulate as he is effusive.

I gratefully accepted their invitation to stay on for dinner and shared in a very pleasant evening of rice, beans, Bible jokes, and movie talk. We were joined by their daughters Skye and Brooke, the farmer on whose land they were now living, and his girlfriend.

I remain impressed with Pastor Paul's sincerity, determination, and courage of conviction.

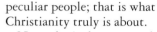

they take the funds that were in the offering box? They confiscated the property and pushed us off. And every time we tried to go back on, our people would get thrown in jail. They tried to pretend as if it was a tax issue, as if the church was to pay taxes to the state for owning property. We were never challenged on the fact that we were a church. They said, and I have it in writing by Marion County officials, attorneys, that this church will, or shall, pay taxes. No other church has to—you see, it's really a privilege granted by the secular government to what they consider "religion."

Pretty much in a nutshell, this sums it all up: we are a church. Literally a church. Church means nation of God, where Jesus Christ is the head. That is by definition what it is. That's what all churches are supposed to be. But those that they think are the church are actually not the church, they are actually harlots, and they have wed the beast. According to anybody that wants to study Revelations. The church is to remain separate and holy. It is to be the unspotted bride of Christ. It is also referred to as the nation of God, peculiar people set apart. We are

peculiar people; that is what Christianity truly is about.

Now why is there so much hate?! Well, because we promote—and this is what the controversy is about—we promote a nation apart from theirs. That's what I want, and I do! We, being separate, we're a threat to what people refer to as the state. Or the States, to the United States.

I've openly declared the Kingdom of Heaven is at hand. And it's God's government. It's the only lawful and legitimate government on the face of the earth. All the rest of the governments are frauds. We're still nationals of the Kingdom of Heaven, we're still citizens. I am not a citizen of the United States. I will *never* claim U.S. citizenship, now that I know who they are and what they are. Never!

So basically, that's our ugly story, if you want to put it that way. It's actually a beautiful story because what it is is that we *are* free, though we have lost in the world—see, those who are in the world would be persecuted. I've hurt no one. Our people have hurt no one. And so without a cause they hated us. If the world loved its own, I mean, they would love us. ■

What does it mean to be an American? Ha ha ha ha. A bunch of people who have fallen asleep who haven't got a clue what's going on. Wake up! It's the final hour, the last hour, midnight. Realize what's going on. The Orwellian concepts are very real. I'm saying as loud as I can, this is *not* a free country. If you want to find out whether you're free or not, you have to test it. Well, we made the test.

> Be strong. Have faith. Be proud of who you are. God made all of us.

eleanor roosevelt

Montrose, Colorado
47 years old

That she cherishes the people in her life is evident in Eleanor's house, which proudly displays pictures of family and friends—her daughter especially—and the drawings, crafts, and other mementos they've given her over the years; and in the way she recounts her favorite experiences. "Have friends instead of money any day," she advised.

I liked the wry tone she'd use to express disbelief as she rolled her eyes: "And I says, oh no . . ." And I was impressed by her honesty and bravery in facing life.

She told me she's often moved to tears at the beauty of the San Juan mountains in her area of western Colorado and that one thing she'd like to do is go to New York and meet Peter Jennings.

I was born in Arizona. I was adopted when I was six. I went to Indian school. And then my foster parents put me in that girls' school. It was like a prison. Nothing but barbed wires around the whole area. I got out of there for good behavior.

When I got adopted I couldn't use my Apache language with my foster parents. They wouldn't understand what I was saying. Plus they'd get upset. So I lost my language. All my sisters and brothers are in Arizona. On the reservation. Last year I went down and I spent Christmas with them. Everyone talks Apache but me. I didn't get close to my family because I had brain damage when I was little. It affected my right side. My hand is crippled.

My life is simple, you know? I stay home a lot. I just try to keep myself busy. Watch TV, the Disney channel and Discovery channel. I keep my house up clean. Everybody says, "Boy, you keep your house really nice . . . " People ask me if I can iron for them. I only charge five dollars. And I clean houses sometimes. I was looking for work but nobody wants to hire handicap people. It makes me feel like I'm *lazy*. I'm trying my best to do my share and I have bills too. Just like anybody else. And sometimes I don't have the money. And sometimes I don't eat. I watch TV and think about other things. I pray. I burn my sage. It's spiritual help, you pray, meditate. And my husband's helping me through the Indian way.

This one dishwashing place gave me a chance and I couldn't keep up. But at least he hired me. "Hey," I says, "maybe I should not work here because I couldn't keep up with the dishes." He said, "Yeah, I think you're right." I said, "One thing I'm thankful for is that you gave me a chance, and I'm very grateful to you." And he was so proud of me, he shook my hand, and he says, "Well, thank you so much," and I left.

I used to be a crossing guard, too. I met my husband on the corner! I liked that job, it was fun. The kids knew me, and they trusted me, you know. But they didn't make fun of me because I was helping them cross the street. One girl said, "Boy, you're the best crossing guard I ever had." I said, "Thank you very much." I said, "That was a nice compliment."

I worry about my daughter a lot. I miss her very much. She's very loving, and she's smart too. I'm full-blooded Apache, and she's half Lakota and half Apache. I'm separated right now. I'm hoping that things will work out with us. Sometimes I have to ask him, I say, please come down—it's hard on him to bring her down. I don't complain that much, but still, I need to see her. I miss 'em both. I still love both of them very much. I don't want to be like my foster parents. They just drifted away. I want her to know I love her. On the phone she told me, "I'm proud to have you for a mom." It was one of those days I had a bad day, and she says, "Mom, don't cry, I'm proud to have you for a mom." I love her to death.

I have a hard time cashing my check now and then. "I need your I.D., ma'am." And I says, oh no, here we go again . . . My grandpa was Franklin Roosevelt. And I already met a Washington. He's a Navajo. He was in Wal-Mart one time, dressed Indian with beads and everything. Finally he said, "My name is Washington." And I says, oh no . . . I guess the Indians like presidents' names. Maybe Navajos or Apaches, I don't know.

I'm proud to be an American Indian. I'm proud to be a mom. I can do a lot of things that people don't see me do. ■

What does it mean to be an American? The Indians were here first, I think the Indians should have more. But you know, most people don't feel that way. More freedom. More housing, more say so, I guess. They need to be treated with more respect, too. The Indians got the bad end of the deal, I think. We should have got more mad. But we didn't. I know there are a lot of black people that got the bad end of the deal too. But you know, I'm not the government. What can I say? I'm just a simple Indian. They won't listen to me. My words won't get anywhere. Unless God listens to me.

What does it mean to be an American? Hmm, that is such a hard one. In Stegner—a wonderful writer about the West—to be an American is to be very connected to others. And I think a lot of that is because the western landscape initially was so foreboding that for people to exist, they learned how to make connections. And yet if you look at a lot of the other American literature, and our whole sense of history, it's to be very independent, very individualistic, so I think we have that split. To be an American is to be individual, is to be independent. And yet it is also to learn to be connected . . . the melting pot.

There are people in this world who are able to, you know, just live life. And then there are the rest of us. Everything that you do, you relive, and you rethink, and you question.

betsy ross

Salt Lake City, Utah
43 years old

Whether it was the enormity of the Utah sky as I drove toward Salt Lake City or the imposing statue of Brigham Young presiding over the rotunda of the State Capitol Building in which Betsy Ross's office was located, I felt I was in a foreign land. Despite the unfamiliar terrain, the Betsy Ross I encountered offered me the incisive advice of a kindred spirit. "I sense you have that creative need too," she said, not five minutes into our meeting. "I hear the split in your life that I've felt in mine and I hope it works for you. I hope you find the right combination." At the time, I was headed off for a job on Wall Street. I knew I'd met a fellow juggler of the conventional and unconventional in this attorney and writer, and that I'd savor the lessons of our conversation.

Betsy's outlook on life drew us into a discussion on existentialism in which in we discovered, in a kismet moment, that the lectures on existentialism I'd been listening to on tape in my car (one has to pass the time) were in fact the recorded lectures of her college philosophy professor.

I am an example—you've probably met many of us—of the new American family. I actually have six kids, because I have two stepchildren with us half-time, week on, week off. The poor kids that are biologically mine are nineteen, seventeen, fifteen, thirteen, and then the two step kids are thirteen and eleven. You *are* in Utah!

Family history? You know, that's a sensitive point, because when I met my ex, I converted to the Mormon religion. My family's Jewish. The Mormon religion has a practice of converting the dead. Their belief—and I say "their" because I've left them—was that you could give those that have already died the opportunity to participate in the gospel by baptizing them, um, after they're dead. That's why genealogy is *so* important to Mormons. Well, my family became aware of that, so information stopped. There was German and Russian descent on my father's side. My mother's side was in Louisiana for a few generations.

I was born in New Orleans. Fun place. My whole family's still back there. I went to the University of Texas in Austin. The conventional route for me, I thought at the time, was going straight to graduate school, or to law school, which is what my parents wanted. So instead, I got a job working for UPS. Well, I am directionally impaired. I was getting lost . . . delivering to residences at eleven o'clock at night. People were sleeping . . . So, off to graduate school in comparative literature. I loved it, I really loved it.

Three years there and then straight out to Salt Lake City. With my husband, ex-husband. He's from here, so we moved back. At that time, there was no Ph.D. program in comparative literature at the University of Utah, so the easiest thing to do was law school. I had three little kids at the time, and I was just going a little bit stir crazy, I think. It wasn't a great

desire to become a lawyer, but . . . it's worked out wonderfully. I have no complaints about being a lawyer, really.

I'm Director of Legal Affairs for the State Auditor and the State Treasurer. Before that I worked as an assistant attorney general, and before that, in the private sector. And before *that*, I clerked for a judge. Having four children and doing the private sector was a difficult road. Many women do it and I certainly respect and admire them; it wasn't me, though. It didn't feel good. This is a way to try to balance the two worlds.

I go home and then it's kids. It's driving kids, it's dinner, it's errands—it's that kind of a life. And if I do that for too long without taking a nice block of time for myself, I go crazy. Particularly if I'm not reading or writing. Often at night, you know, after I've been with them during the day, I don't feel any guilt about taking a couple of hours and closing the door to my little reading room. I publish book reviews for the Utah Bar Journal. Prior to that, I wrote book reviews for a weekly newspaper. And if I don't run at least three days a week, I'll start feeling like a slug, too. So I run, I mountain bike, I ski during ski season—advantages of being out west. Isn't it beautiful? I just feel like I have the West in my soul.

I know very little about Betsy Ross, but the interesting point is that it is very much a part of me. For example, when I first married, I took my ex-husband's name. When we divorced, I took my name back, and when I remarried, I kept my name. Ross is my maiden name. I like to say that it has kept me from being shy, and I think it has, because so many people comment on it, you find yourself having to say something in return . . . It creates an automatic bridge between people. That's probably what I've enjoyed more than anything else. ∎

God I was tough, wasn't I? I wasn't afraid of anything.

babe ruth

Lansing, Michigan
84 years old

Asked if she has anything in common with her famous namesake, Babe answered, "Well, I guess we're both characters." Absolutely! Babe (officially, Marion "Babe" Weyant Ruth) was my last interview after two months on the road. Talking with her was the perfect wrap-up to the trip.

After talking at her home, we set off for the airport down the road to take her portrait. Everybody knew Babe by name and waved us in. As we were setting up the photo, Babe heard a plane coming in and instinctively turned with delight to the sky.

We went to one of her old haunts for dinner—a porterhouse steak apiece—and then popped by another restaurant a friend of hers ran for a piece of pie. Everywhere we went, I heard, Babe! Hey Babe! This tiny, practical, and irreverent woman is something of a legend in Lansing, as in the aviation world. One of five female pilot instructors in World War II, she's earned a number of prestigious flying awards, including Michigan Aviation Hall of Fame and the 99's Lifetime Achievement Award. And she showed me the personal letter she'd received from Amelia Earhart in 1933.

Babe put me up for the night in her guest room, and insisted on getting up and fixing me eggs before I left early the next morning for New York.

Rottweiler. I won't let her in because she'll love you to death. One of the airport cops gave her to me. 'Cause my husband, you know, died last—two years ago. Oh, God, she's a lot of company. And she darn fool understands English, too.

My folks called me Baby, then shortened it to Babe. My mother—now don't laugh—called me Cle-ola Arlene. Cleola Arlene. So that's about all the excitement there was till I got married.

I spent my life at this airport—since I was ten years old. We moved out here when I was in the fourth grade. Dad was a telephone man, and my mother always worked. They didn't know what to do with me when they went into town. So they'd drop me off at the airport. So I'd sit there on the cornerstone and occasionally an airplane would come in. I've seen it go from a 2000-foot gravel runway to what it is today.

All the fellas looked after me. I mean, they raised me. When the guys were home on the air show circuit, you see, they would teach me to fly. My dad didn't know. So one day he stopped there to fix the telephone and they wanted to know when I was going to solo.

You had to be sixteen. My mother signed my license. I soloed on Navy day. October the twenty-seventh. I was working in the restaurant and Harvey come over, he says, "Let's go take a fly." So I put my coat on, on top of my apron. I hung onto him. I wasn't going to let him out. He says, "Now if you bounce," he says, "open the throttle and drop the nose." I didn't bounce.

I have a personal letter from Amelia Earhart. Before I started to fly, I wrote and asked her what I could do to learn to fly so she wrote me back, and I've got the letter. I had an airplane when I was nineteen. See, I didn't drive a car till I was twenty-five years old.

World War II, I said I'm more important as an instructor than as a pilot. During the war, I was a civilian instructor for air transport command. I've taught a lot of people here to fly in Lansing, including the doctor that delivered both of my children—till I got sick in '93.

I had a stroke, and then, two years later, open-heart surgery. My husband and I took turns going to Emergency. He died on his birthday. Seventy-seven. I was five years older than he. So don't let 'em tell you that they don't work, because we were married fifty-three years. Dale told me the only reason he married me 'cause I could hunt and fish. The only reason I married him so I could be Babe Ruth!

We drove to Alaska for over twenty years till my husband got sick. We stayed in hunting camps. I liked to say, I slept with a lot of strange men, but I never slept with a rifle until I went to Alaska. When you got grizzlies coming into camp, you sleep with a rifle right beside you, loaded. All we ate for twenty years is moose. By the time you go up there and buy a license, that darn thing costs about three hundred dollars a pound.

Am I happy? No I'm *not*, 'cause I don't have my husband. I'm not unhappy. I just miss *him*, that's all.

God, I don't know what I'm proud of . . . Being married fifty-three years. Having two good-looking daughters. And three smart grandchildren. 'Course you never forget the first solo.

I know people tell me I led an interesting life. Well, that's just the way my folks were. You know, we weren't rich or anything. But we did things together. My dad never went deer hunting unless he took my mother and I with him. We went with him to everything. But anyway, I haven't had a dull life. ∎

What does it mean to be an American? I don't know, I've never been anything else but.

What does it mean to be an American? Well, I'm proud to be an American. But we've let too many in here and it's ruining our country. It's hard to get 'em out if they get in. Send 'em to school down in—what was it down in Florida where they was training 'em to fly? Training 'em to tear up our country. That's pretty bad. I don't think it's ever gonna be back like it was, d'you?

> If somebody tells you what to do and how to do it, see if they've made a success out of it. If they have, listen to 'em. And if they haven't, don't you listen!

homer simpson

Loudon, Tennessee
74 years old

Homer Simpson was giving me directions to his dairy farm over the phone: "You'll make a right when you get to the second silo . . ." "Third silo!" I heard a voice yell in the background. It was Sue Simpson—affectionately known as "Mama"—baker of the most delicious, melt-in-your-mouth biscuits you could ever hope to taste.

"Did you see that fire truck we sent to New York?" Mr. Simpson asked when I arrived, referring to Knoxville's gift in the aftermath of 9/11. I enjoyed his rich stories and the casual banter we developed. He chided that I'd be an old maid if I didn't hurry up. And he cracked me up as I took his picture, muttering, "I don't know why a city girl would be wasting all that time and film on a bunch of east Tennessee hillbillies . . ."

We was raised the rough way. And I'm proud of it. Born three-tenths of a mile from here. On the right, at the end of the road. That's as far as I got. To the poorhouse and stopped! The county used to own this farm and they called it the poor farm. They kept the paupers in the two little houses up there on the hill. And when they sold it, my daddy bought it. The auctioneer got up on a fifty-five gallon drum here in the yard and auctioned it off.

Growin' up, they called me Muddy Foot. See, we had to walk to school, rain, sleet or snow, and the old road didn't have any gravel on it. And I guess I didn't go around too many of the mud puddles. Used to be a great big tree up on the hill and when we went to church on Sunday, we'd hide our old shoes up there, and put our good shoes on and go on to town. And then when we'd come back we'd put our old shoes on and carry our good shoes home. That's how muddy the road was.

Mother, she was a worker. They had to make her quit driving the tractor when she was eighty-something years old. She'd bale hay, anything. She was a better worker'n Daddy. She was a character. One year Daddy and Mother decided not to vote because they would just kill each other's votes. He slipped off and walked to town and voted. Daddy was a Republican, so right after we were married, Mother took us and registered us Democrats.

Homer Simpson . . . I guess everybody knows me for that now. It's been twelve or fifteen years since that program come on, isn't it? That's when we got to having trouble. They used to call all during the night: "Is Bart there?" I finally figured out that it was on television. I never had seen it. Don't care nothing about tele-

vision, just the ballgames. People got to bring me undershirts with the Simpsons on it and everything so it finally soaked in the hard head. It don't bother me.

I get out and help the boys with what I can do. I drive the tractor, things I can do sittin' down, run the wagon, help 'em load the sileage. But I'm getting where I can't do too much. We've got seventy-five head of beef cattle and eighty-five or ninety head of dairy cattle. This time of year, we come in about five or six o'clock. And when the weather's fit, we come in at eight or nine o'clock then. With all we've got to do. It's going rougher every year. The big man just strips the little man out. We're still holding our head above water, though; just praying we hit the bottom.

I just worry about it staying in farming when I die. If the boys don't have the money to pay inheritance, all they can do is sell it. And it's not fair—'cause they made a lot of it theirself. That's all they've ever done. So, it just sort of puts a bind on what's best to do. You know, if it's yours, it's yours. You hate somebody take it away from you.

I'm proud of that old scissors, my wife. I'm proud I've done as good as I have. Built this house and didn't have any money. My daddy said, "The poor bum's going crazy. He's building a house big enough for a tobacco warehouse." But we worked and we saved and we paid it off. It's not what you make, it's what you save . . . I never have borrowed any money, don't have any credit rating. I charge all I want to at the co-op. That's all I need. As long as I got a top over me and somethin' to eat, I'm happy.

I don't worry about anything, just getting old. I just I sit here in my chair and sleep, don't I, Mama? Yeah, I prop up and go to sleep. ■

Easy things are hard for me. And hard things are easy.

joan sitting bull

Bosque Farms, New Mexico
50 years old

Admittedly, I didn't expect Joan Sitting Bull to be a white woman, but then, whoever opened the door was never as I imagined—and that's by far the best part of this project. And what a jewel I found in Joan Sitting Bull.

Although extremely busy, Joan agreed to meet at the Church's restaurant she manages at nine-thirty in the evening—once they'd closed the doors and were operating only on drive-thru. She bought me dinner and we sat out front, joined by Frank Lopez, the Market Leader for the six Church's stores in the region. She is at once intense and friendly, quick and deliberate, tough and deferential, strong and spiritual.

Joan Sitting Bull clearly cares about the tasks before her and the people around her, and she leads by example. Her eyes are penetrating and her laugh spontaneous.

I took this photo of her the following afternoon as she worked the drive-thru window.

I, a female, a white female, have the Sitting Bull name, and I can speak the spiritual language. I married into it; I divorced out of it. He was the great grandson of Chief Sitting Bull, a Vietnam veteran that was a prisoner of war. He had every disc in his back broken by the Vietnamese. An old oriental man put a ladder up against him and put herbs on his back, and that's how he managed to survive. He was one of the first few that came out when Nixon opened the door and got the prisoners out. I became more of a Sitting Bull than he was. So when we separated, I kept the name. Sitting Bull is what was given to me, and it must remain.

I'm a very strong person, very strong-willed. I'm not one of your naïve, young, frail things that's gonna say, "Go ahead, bust my face," because buddy, you come and bust my face, I may bust your face back. So am I afraid? Yeah. Am I gonna care? No. I raised three children by myself, three boys. I have fought gangs, myself, to claim back my home, to claim back my children, one at a time. With the good Lord's help every now and then somebody would jump in, but I knew if they were there, time was limited. It might be a week, it might be a day, but then I would have to pick up the slats and go again. I feel, like everyone else. But I do it in my own way.

My mom has a great saying: you've got ten minutes to cry and get over it and get back to work. Life is this way. There's not a rose garden for people, knights in shining armor. Those things don't happen. There's a lot of fairy tales that we create in our own mind, but get over it. W-O-R-K is exactly what it takes.

I started out at sixteen in Walgreen's restaurant. I've worked mostly in the man's fields.

Roofing, construction, you name it. So I experienced a lot in life and the circle brought me back to food. Food is where I like to be, working with the public, treating people the way that I like to be treated, the old-fashioned way. The grace of the Creator brought me to Church's. Had I heard of Church's? Kind of. Did I ever think about working at Church's? No. I never dreamed I'd ever work in fast food. And I'll tell you what, the Creator knows exactly what He does and He put me in positions, places and times, exactly where I needed to be.

When I first came here, I thought I was pretty experienced. These people were running circles around me. Frank, the training manager, gave me two weeks of training and then he threw me to the wolves. One million, one billion times I was gonna quit. There ain't no doubt about it. But I didn't. And here I am. I have worked awful hard to get here.

Church's helped pay for part of my tuition to go to school, and I decided to go and get my degree in business administration. So I go to school part time, I work full time. To go to school and to run a high-volume store and to live a life and be a part of the community—it is a challenge. Seven or eight in the morning till eleven or twelve at night. And if something happens in the day, it could be one o'clock in the morning. Then, by the time I get home, twenty-five miles away, it's a lot later than that. It's a mindset: this is what you have to do. You better take your vitamins, your protein!

Attitude and determination is what makes it possible for anyone—myself or anyone—to move forward. You betcha. Give me a chance. Watch me fly. I have so much strength and so much energy, the best is yet to come. ∎

What does it mean to be an American? We have everything. I try not to take advantage of it, I try not to waste water, I try not to take advantage of just having all these wonderful things that other people dream about or strive for and wish that they had, but, for whatever reason, they don't. I feel very fortunate.

What does it mean to be an American? **I'm proud to be an American.**

It's come a long way in ninety-eight years.

gertrude stein

Rensselaer, Indiana
98 years old

I arrived on a Sunday, the day Gertrude Stein's daughter Janice visited. Fortunately for me, Janice stayed to help facilitate the conversation, repeating my questions for her mother when I wasn't sufficiently clear or loud, and helping jog her memory. Mrs. Stein spoke fondly and frequently of having Janice when she was forty-nine, and of her recent ninety-eighth birthday party. Her side of the nursing home room was colorful, its wall fully covered with family photos, cards, and drawings.

I particularly enjoyed the banter she and her nurse, Martha, shared. I think it was the only time she cracked a smile during the photo shoot. Nurse Martha provoked her with, "She's too nice to be your daughter, as ornery as you are, Ms. Gertrude," to which Gertrude replied, "Well, you stinker, you!"

The twenty-second of March was my birthday. I was ninety-eight that day. It was on a Friday, the twenty-second.

They had a big birthday party for me. The party was on Sunday at my daughter's home in Remington and the whole family came: kids and grandkids and great-grandkids. Thirteen grandchildren, if I'm not mistaken. Fifteen great-grandkids. She baked my birthday cake and she put a picture, my baby picture, on.

I was the first girl. My dad just said, "Oh, we finally got a girl!" There were a bunch of us. They had three boys and then three girls. I'm the only one left.

I taught school four years in one-room country schools around Remington. And I then I got married and had a baby that next year, 1921, so I had to quit teaching. In those days we didn't have babysitters like they do now.

They had barn dances around out in the country every week. And I think when I first saw him, it was at Bud Smith's and he jumped out the window. I thought he was kind of crazy, but he got my attention.

We lived on one farm for thirty-nine years. Mm hmm. Oats and corn, also raised a bunch of chickens. 'Bout the first of April we got five hundred new chickens, every year. And then we had to put papers on the floor and see that each chicken got his head in some water, got a drink of water, and then they'd just run around till we got them all watered. And then we'd just take care of 'em . . .

They say, "You ever milked cows?" I said, "I've milked too many of them!" That's why my hands are so numb. I have arthritis in my hands and in my feet real bad. Yes, it was all by hand—no milkers. It was tough, but it just was part of living.

I was forty-nine years old when I had her. I had a girl and two boys and I kept praying I would get another little girl and, well, if it's not to be, I'll take what I got and be happy . . . And then nineteen years later, I had her. And we all loved her. We brought her home from the hospital, Robert wanted to hold her in the backseat. And it was cold and I had an old Ford and I said no, but he scooted up out of the backseat and had his head in between us.

"Ohhh," some of the neighbors, they said, "How are you going to take care of her?" I says, "Well, like I took care of the rest of them. You don't forget." They said, "How's she going to take care of that baby when she hasn't had one for nineteen years?" I said, "I'll make it." And I did pretty good with her.

I've been here about a little over a year, haven't I? . . . Since '97? I get up, and have breakfast, and sometimes they take you for therapy. Come back and just watch television if I don't have anything on my mind. I like ballgames. I always liked the Cubs, I always wanted to go see 'em. Didn't get to.

She's a big help. She comes every week and stays with me and takes my clothes home and washes them, brings them back. She comes every Sunday to see me. I look forward to seeing her come.

Sometimes I just put a couple pillows on my lap and take a nap. My daughter from Indianapolis calls me every night at four o'clock. Because if you get in bed, they get so busy they can't always come and get you out. So if I falls asleep on my lap, I'm up when she calls. She calls me every day at four o'clock. From Indianapolis.

I guess I'll be here till I die. I'd rather be home. But I'm here and they all come to see me and they all send me things. And that means a lot. We got a strong family. ∎

You can do whatever you want to do.

shirley temple

Brooklyn, New York
66 years old

When I reached Shirley Temple by phone, she agreed to talk with me—as long as it wasn't from eight to ten p.m., the hours she watches her telenovelas. In a welcome change, I walked right past my car for this interview and hopped the subway a quick two stops down the line (never mind that I mistook the express train for the local and had to double back, now late . . .).

We sat down in her beautiful living room, underneath photos of children and grandchildren, all of whom she introduced by name and referred to throughout our conversation. The room also boasted a formidable doll collection, which she'd begun thirty years ago with the little yellow doll that came with margarine back then.

I had the pleasure of meeting her daughters Sandy and Michelle and her granddaughter Gabriela. Asked to describe their mother, Michelle talked of her mother's dedication to helping people who need a hand up, calling to mind something Mrs. Temple told me: "Your problem is my problem. I'll try to solve your problem if I can." And Sandy added, "She's our fortress. Mother, father; she's our strength."

I was born in Panama City. I came to New York 1967. I was thirty-two. Straight to Brooklyn. Been here ever since. My sister came first, then my brother, and then myself. Then my baby brother came.

I knew I wanted to *do* something to make a better living for my kids. By myself, one parent. I just *had* to. Whatever you want to be here in New York, you can be. Just go for it. And that's exactly what I did. You'd say, if she can do this, so can I. But I'll do it my way. Yeah? So I did. I made it. I knew what I wanted, so I went for it and I got it.

When I first got here I lived with a girl-friend. My second paycheck, I decided I'm going on my own. Within three years I sent for my kids. I knew they had the potential and could make a better life here than back home. And they all did end up being productive citizens, because every one of them has gotten a good education—I stressed education—and they have a profession. Three of them are teachers, and a paralegal. My son, he works for the transit as a mechanic. And the other one passed away, he had kidney failure. He was a diabetic.

I was surprised because they did very well in school the first year after they were here. But see, my parents, they spoke a lot of English in the house. So this is where they picked up English. Because my father used to give them the newspaper, because he's from the Canal Zone and he reads the newspaper in English, so he'd give it to them and tell them to read it: "Now explain to me, what did you read?" Good for him *and* them, that they were able to come here and go ahead and make it here. Now they love it. It's a better living for them.

I took courses in English and then I went to Staten Island Community College. I'd get up at four in the morning, cook, go to work, I had to be on the job at seven, get off at three. Go straight to Staten Island—we'd communicate by phone, all through the day I'd be calling them. Now do this, don't do that, do this, do that, is everybody in? I'd get home nine-thirty, ten o'clock, *eleven* o'clock sometimes. I was trying to get a career in nursing. But then when time came for my practical, I couldn't do it, because I had no other income and I needed an income. So I took the phlebotomy and I took the EKG technician.

I worked there for twenty-seven years, at New York Eye and Ear. I retired as a phlebotomist, EKG technician, ahead of time because I was very sick. Cancer in '94. The doctor told my kids to go home and make preparations to bury me. The doctors don't know why, but here I am to tell the tale. Miraculously. God has been very good to me.

I'm a finance minister and a eucharistic minister. And Health Club and Rosary Society, past president. I'm not working per se, to get a paycheck, but I go to my church every day and help at the food pantry. We distribute food. Just two of us. So I go there Monday, Tuesday, Wednesday, and Thursday, from one to four. Only Friday we don't have pantry. Mrs. Faye Buchanan and Shirley Temple, those are the two volunteers. Thanksgiving we feed over three hundred people. For sit down.

Yes, my mother did name me after Shirley Temple. I was never married. So I kept the name. When I go to Macy's and I hand them my card, they always say, "Is *that* your name?!?" Then I'll say—because of course her name is Shirley Temple Black—"I'm the black Shirley Temple." ∎

112

What does it mean to be an American? I'm proud to be one, very proud. This is a big melting pot. You find people from all over. And whatever you want to be you can be. That's what I taught my children. And see, they all did it.

martha washington

New Orleans, Louisiana
86 years old

I'm from New Orleans, only New Orleans. I've been on this block forty-eight years. Twenty-one years I was custodian at the same school. My dad was born here and my mother was born in Pearlington; that's in Slidell. My grandmother and my grandfather was from here. And they was, like, mixed up, Indian or something. My grandfather was a dark man, like me.

I have a friend, she tells people, "I know a colored girl named Martha Washington." And they say, *"Noooo . . ."* She says she's gonna have to bring them by the house.

My husband had a cousin named George Washington. He was walking out of this store on Canal Street and I was going in. So he said, "Hi, sister." So I said, "Hi, man"—I call a lot of people "man," or "girl," or "honey." So the clerk say, "Mr. Washington, you see this lady coming in? If you guess her name, I'll buy you a pair of shoes." So he said, "Martha Washington." "Aaaah, Mr. Washington, I never knew you was going to guess!" He said, "That's my cousin's wife." She was laughing, "Oh, no! We have a George Washington and Martha Washington here!" And they had a write-up in the *Times-Picayune*. It was kicks that day! It was something, hidy ho! But she sure didn't give me *my* shoes half price or nothing. I had to pay all of mine . . . Heh heh heh.

My maiden name was Blue. Unh huh, and all the children would call me by my full name: "Hey, Martha Blue!" I didn't like that at all. My uncle and my aunt, they had a buggy—they had a little fifteen cents, too, I mean a little money. On Sundays and holidays when I'd be in that buggy, the children would holler, "Hey, Martha Blue!" and I wouldn't answer. My aunt would say, "Unh unh, we don't play that selfish stuff in here"—because very few people had a buggy. "You hear that girl?" And I'd say, "Oh, *hiiiiii,*

Mrs. Washington was ill in bed when I arrived for the interview, so we decided I'd return the following morning. When I did, I accidentally woke and then displaced her visiting grandson, who'd been asleep on the couch in the front room. Friends and neighbors popped in and rang throughout the morning.

"Didn't I tell you she could talk?" her grandson asked hours later, joining his grandmother on the front steps to see me off. She is indeed full of stories and has a rare gift of delivery—conspiratorial whisper and all. When I embraced her goodbye, headed for the Arkansas border, she chuckled, "Oooo, now I have two white girls that come and hug me." (Her nurse is the other.) I enjoyed myself thoroughly, thrilled I'd found this Martha Washington.

I called her the other day, just to check in, and she proudly reported she'd just made eighty-seven!

114

I pray and ask the Lord to give me my health and don't let me go senile. My mama died with her good senses and I want to die with mine.

my mind was gone." My aunt made me. When I'd be in that buggy I thought I was somebody.

I have four girls living and one boy. I lost a girl and I lost a boy. Nineteen grandchildren and I think ten great-grandchildren and one great-great. A little girl had fun, she said, "Well, you must be a hundred and something, you got a daughter older than my grandma!" Lord, that was cute. I must be a hundred and some years old! That do sound funny, *I have a daughter sixty-seven* . . . I'm proud of my children 'cause they're good to me. So I say I'm some blessed.

The other day I was counting my bills and I told this one, "I'm short on money." So he says, "I'll give you this hundred and I ain't giving you no more"—because I play the slots. I told him I play the nickel ones—*but I play the quarters* . . . One day I lost three hundred and sixty dollars. I couldn't sleep that night. I asked my daughter if she had a nerve pill. Sure enough, I had to take one. And about four o'clock that morning I said, "Oh, my bill money!" I took another one. I would have some money if I wouldn't be playing.

Worries? Oh, every little thing. Like if they go out at night. Like now if he be on the water. There was this boy on the ship, and he ain't take no foolishness from white or black. So he was kind of sassy, and he was a cook, and they said he run out the door and fell in the water. And the sharks ate him. Now you know better than that. That boy didn't run off. People say them white boys throwed him in the water. So I be, you know, scared plenty. I tell them they've got to be careful . . . it's good that they got these little phones.

I was worried about my insurance, 'cause I only have four thousand and five hundred and my son, he told me, "Don't worry, I'm gonna give you four thousand on your funeral"—'cause six thousand and five hundred could bury you,

you know. One of my friends' caskets cost eight thousand dollars. Ooooo, it looked like pearl and the handles like gold. Say she'll last for a hundred years. What good is it going to do? They ain't going to open that thing up! I think that was foolish. I mean and her suit, I know her suit cost about three hundred dollars. It was beautiful. So I got a blue one. My daughter paid, I think, a hundred and twenty-nine dollars. It's embroidered. So I don't have to worry.

The onlyest thing I'd want is a little sewing machine, I had one but it was old. My old big sew good till I would hate to give it up, but it's no kind of old, it's old. On the side . . . part of that fell off . . . You've got to be careful because that tin'll scratch you. You know that'll cut your clothes, so you got to be careful when you pass. I had taped it, but when the tape go warm it came aloose. So I've got to get some real glue. So that's about the onlyest thing I crave. Because we got TV for all the rooms and we got the tapes.

My day? I read my Bibles and my newspaper. I go on the front porch and read the paper and come back. Early in the morning I say my prayers and I drink my coffee. Full day of church on Wednesdays. And the rest of the time, I just watch TV. I don't walk enough. I have a stick but I just don't have energy. I just feel tired. My feets are swollen, see? Doctor said that's fluid. And I got like arthritis or something. And my gallstones are hurting. I forget the vice president's name . . . What the vice president had, this is that.

I was gone twice. They shocked my heart twice. Eight months ago. I was eighty-five; I'm eighty-six now. "Sister's some sick and we don't know if she's gonna make it!" They call me Sister, grandchildren and all. The doctor say I pulled through it fine because the Lord wasn't ready for me. ∎

What does it mean to be an American? Oh, everything to me. Because I was born here. You're free here. That's why I like America.

"You can't always get what you want, but you get what you need." Make the most of whatever you've got.

john wayne

Phillips, Nebraska
50 years old

My meetings with John provided visual feasts in two completely different realms that rainy, gray Nebraska spring day. Wayne Cyclery is located in a giant downtown Grand Island building whose history includes time as a black USO in World War I, a bus station in the day of horse-drawn buses, and a bar. It now houses more bikes than you could imagine in any one place.

That evening, I joined him at his home at feeding time for his motley assortment of animals. I had a blast watching and photographing as horses, llamas, dogs, and a goose vied for John's attention.

I was also impressed by his stories of his parents' support and example, and his advice to get out and explore your interests in life before settling down with someone who also shares them. Something he's content he did.

It's great out here. We can see sunsets. A lot of older people actually are retiring to the Midwest. It's quieter, you know, it's a bit slower life. I'll do a delivery to one of these small towns, and you drop it off and you have to sit there and have coffee and cookies for an hour before they'll let you leave.

I went to school and got an architecture degree. I was gonna go to graduate school, become a landscape architect. I couldn't really afford to go to school and work and live. At the time, I was working in a bike shop and I really enjoyed it, so I kind of continued working there. And after several years it was like, well, if I'm running this shop for somebody else, I can do it myself.

So I came out here in '81, bought a building, just committed myself. That first year I sold forty-five bikes. I was starving—eating a lot of rice. I sat on a chair in this empty building. And I was in *tears* a few times. *God,* you know, *I'm gonna to fail . . .* The first years were starvation, but after that, it started getting better and better. Now we sell over a thousand bikes a year.

People are overwhelmed when they come in here, because it's 650 bikes in here—middle of Nebraska. Most of our customers are within fifty, sixty miles away. It's a slow enough pace that people can just come in, talk with us—we don't force anybody to buy anything, but we've got what they want.

Everybody who works here, we all do it 'cause it's fun. We could be doing lots of other things but we like getting our hands dirty and riding bikes. From nine o'clock in the morning till six, six-thirty—it's fixing bikes, showing people new bikes. Tuesdays and Thursdays, if the weather's nice, a bunch of us go bike riding. You got to do what you enjoy doing.

At the house, we've got a huge garden that we take care of. We've got potatoes, carrots, peas, tomatoes, radishes. I can't go to a grocery store and buy a tomato. Vegetables taste better if you grow 'em yourself.

We have all kinds of animals—horses, llamas, turkeys—actually we have just one turkey, he's kind of lonesome—we have three dogs, too many cats. And more llamas every year: Franklin here, he seems to get Glenda pregnant every year.

One goose, we raised it from an egg and it seems to think I'm its surrogate mother. He has to follow me when I do the chores in the morning; it's embarrassing sometimes, you turn around and there's this goose you're tripping over. The dogs are the only animals that are allowed in the house. So mornings, I get up, have a cup of coffee and go out and feed the animals . . . John Wayne? Yeah! We both have love for animals, and horses. For a while the comment was I looked more like John Denver.

The September eleventh thing changed life a lot. Before that, I worried a lot about how the kids were turning out, what they were doing wrong, or what they were doing that I didn't approve of. Since then, it's don't worry about the small things, and they're all small things. Life goes on, and no matter what you do, you'll live through it, so. Everything works out in the end. What's it help to worry?

I think there's a lot of things going wrong with the world, but there's a lot of things going right with the world too. And you need to start thinking about those, dwelling on those, things that everybody's doing right instead of the things that everybody's doing wrong.

I'm proud of the business. I have a good life. I stay pretty busy. My theory is: as long as you have projects, you can't die. So I figure, I'm good for two, three hundred years. ∎

What does it mean to be an American? You're an American and it gives you all these rights, but you also have responsibilities that go along with those rights. For the most part, we've got a pretty good country here.

famous names, famous people

John Adams (1735–1826). Vice president to George Washington and second president of the United States. A profound political thinker, Adams helped draft the Declaration of Independence. Until recently, he was the only president whose son (John Quincy Adams) also served as president.

Samuel Adams (1722–1803). Revolutionary War leader and Boston radical, Adams helped organize the Sons of Liberty and plan the Boston Tea Party. One of the original signers of the Declaration of Independence, Adams also ultimately helped ratify the Constitution.

Muhammad Ali (born Cassius Clay, 1942–). Three-time boxing heavyweight champion of the world, Ali is also known for his flamboyant personality and witty self-promotion: "I am the greatest." "I float like a butterfly and sting like a bee." Ali converted to the Nation of Islam and refused to be drafted into the army, citing religious reasons. His subsequent conviction was overturned by the Supreme Court.

Clara Barton (1821–1912). Founder of the American Red Cross, Barton was most famous for her humanitarian work in the Civil War, serving as superintendent of nurses for the Union army. She served as president of the Red Cross from 1882 to 1904.

Al Capone (1899–1947). Gang boss during Prohibition whose empire included control of the bootleg whiskey market, as well as gambling, prostitution, and dance halls in Chicago. Two years after Capone's "St. Valentine Day's Massacre," claiming the lives of seven members of the rival Bugs Moran gang, Capone was arrested for tax evasion and spent eight years in Alcatraz.

Charlie Chaplin (1889–1977). Chaplin made his name as a silent movie star, known for his comic genius and versatility. During the Red Scare, his left-wing politics were unpopular in the United States and he was banned from reentering the country until 1972, when he received an honorary Oscar for his pioneering work.

Cesar Chavez (1927–1993). Agricultural labor leader, Chavez was a Mexican-American migrant farm worker who spoke out to improve conditions for farm workers. In 1962 he established the National Farm Workers Association, later called the United Farm Workers, in California. He was an advocate of nonviolent protest.

Christopher Columbus (1451–1506). Portuguese explorer who crossed the Atlantic Ocean under the auspices of King Ferdinand and Queen Isabella of Spain and "discovered" America in 1492. He landed in the islands of the Caribbean while searching for a sea route west to the riches of Asia.

Davy Crockett (1786–1836). Frontiersman, soldier, congressman, and folk hero, Crockett was a versatile legend and a tall storyteller. Crockett died defending the Alamo, after losing a reelection bid for Congress.

James Dean (1931–1955). Actor who starred in only three films, *Rebel without a Cause*, *East of Eden*, and *Giant*, before dying in a tragic car accident at twenty-four. His portrayals of troubled, moody young men made him a lasting icon of rebellious youth.

Emily Dickinson (1830–1886). Poet known for her precise and simple language. A reclusive poet, treating themes of nature and existential truth, she composed roughly 1,700 poems, only ten of which were published during her lifetime.

Frederick Douglass (1818–1895). Douglass escaped from slavery in 1838 in Baltimore to become a spokesman, protester, and author fighting against slavery, racism, and unjust laws. After releasing his autobiography, *Narrative of the Life of Frederick Douglass*, Douglass took sanctuary in England before his freedom was bought in 1847.

Bob Dylan (born Robert Zimmerman, 1941–). Musician whose music encompassed rock, country, Christian, and folk, Dylan is best known for his lyrics—many of which contain political and moral sentiments. His most famous songs include "Blowin' in the Wind" and "The Times They Are A-Changin'."

Amelia Earhart (1897–1937). Aviator and feminist. Earhart was the first woman to fly solo across the Atlantic Ocean. Attempting to fly around the world in 1937, her plane disappeared over the Pacific Ocean and was never recovered.

Betty Ford (born Elizabeth Bloomer, 1918–). During her tenure as first lady to thirty-eighth president Gerald Ford, she focused on arts, handicapped children and women's issues and was involved with working toward the passage of the Equal Rights Amendment. She is best known for her active work improving awareness, education, and treatment of alcohol and other chemical dependencies and for her work founding and running the outstanding treatment facility that bears her name.

Greta Garbo (born Greta Gustafsson, 1905–1990). Highly successful Swedish-born U.S. actress who performed in twenty-seven films, both silent and sound, from 1922 to 1941. Her intense need for privacy led her to withdraw from the limelight and retire into obscurity without explanation at the height of her career.

Jerry Garcia (1942–1995). Rock musician and artist. Best known as lead guitarist and vocalist for the Grateful Dead. This San Francisco group enjoyed popularity over decades, spawning an entire counter-cultural phenomenon of loyalists called Deadheads.

Al Gore, Jr. (1948–). Two-term vice president of the United States under Bill Clinton. Gore became known as a strong spokesman for environmental and technology issues. Gore won the popular vote in his 2000 bid for the presidency, but lost the election to George W. Bush on electoral college votes. Gore's father, Albert Gore, Sr., was a congressman and senator for over thirty years.

Jimmy Hoffa (1913–1975?). President of the Teamsters Union, Hoffa secured the first national trucking contract in the union's history. Renowned as a leader, Hoffa successfully defended corruption charges, but was indicted for tampering and misusing union funds. After eight years in jail, he returned to take control of the union, but disappeared. Though never found, he is presumed to have been murdered.

Oliver Wendell Holmes, Sr. (1809–1894). Author, physician, and dean at Harvard Medical School, Holmes was best known for his witty poems, essays, and novels, including "Old Ironsides." Holmes's writings on proper hygiene during childbirth are credited with saving countless lives. His son, Oliver Wendell Holmes, Jr. (1841–1935), known as "the Great Dissenter," was chief justice of the Massachusetts Supreme Court and a liberal associate justice of the U.S. Supreme Court.

Herbert Hoover (1874–1964). Thirty-first president of the United States from 1929 to 1933, during the Great Depression. Hoover was criticized for his inability to pull the nation out of the Depression and was soundly defeated by Franklin D. Roosevelt in '32.

Rock Hudson (born Roy Scherer, 1925–1985). Actor who epitomized Hollywood's dashing leading man of the 1950's and '60's. His announcement that he was dying of AIDS raised awareness of the disease.

Langston Hughes (1902–1967). African-American author, poet, and playwright. Perhaps best known for his poetry, Hughes was a major figure in the Harlem Renaissance of the 1920's, writing of the black experience in America.

Jesse James (1847–1882). Outlaw leader of the James gang, which robbed banks, trains, and coaches, and long-eluded the Pinkerton detectives. Gang member Robert Ford shot Jesse James in the head to collect a reward of $5,000 that was posted for his death.

Thomas Jefferson (1743–1826). Third president of the United States, Jefferson is regarded as a statesman and intellectual, an inventor, musician, architect, and agriculturalist. He is most famous for writing the Declaration of Independence.

Helen Keller (1880–1968). Author, educator, and rights activist, Keller lost her sight and hearing to scarlet fever at nineteen months. With the help of her teacher, Anne Sullivan, she overcame her disabilities to graduate from Radcliffe College, where she learned to both read and write Braille. She wrote and lectured widely on the plight of the handicapped.

Grace Kelly (1928–82). Fifties film actress and Princess of Monaco, whose acclaimed films include *Fourteen Hours*, *High Noon*, *The Country Girl,* and Hitchcock classics. Her movie career ended in 1956 when she married Prince Rainier III of Monaco. She died in an automobile crash.

Jacquelyn Kennedy (Onassis) (1929–1994). A very popular First Lady, married to John F. Kennedy. They married in 1953 while John F. Kennedy was a senator and she was a photojournalist for the *Washington Times Herald*. In the White House she was known for her elegance, style, and charm, setting international fashion trends. In 1968 she married Aristotle Onassis.

John F. Kennedy (1917–1963). Thirty-fifth president of the United States, Kennedy narrowly defeated Nixon to become the youngest and first Roman Catholic president. Kennedy pushed for educational assistance, health care, and civil rights legislation. Kennedy was widely seen as charismatic and intelligent, and his assassination on November 22, 1963, allegedly by Lee Harvey Oswald, shook the nation.

Martin Luther King, Jr. (1929–1968). Ordained Baptist minister and nonviolent civil rights activist. Dr. King founded the Southern Christian Leadership Conference to combat racism and segregation. An orator of great renown, he delivered his most famous speech, "I Have a Dream," on the steps of the Lincoln Memorial during the 1963 March on Washington. King was assassinated on April 4th, 1968.

Lois Lane. Fictional character in the Superman stories. The *Daily Planet*'s star reporter, Lane is Superman's love interest.

Bruce Lee (1940–1973). Actor and martial artist of great reknown. Lee had an extensive film career in Hong Kong before his breakthrough in the U.S. with in the television series *The Green Hornet*. Lee's American film classics include *Fists of Fury*, *Game of Death,* and *Enter the Dragon.*

Robert E. Lee (1807–1870). Confederate Civil War general, known for both his military genius and his personal integrity. Lee was offered the command of the Union army but chose to side with Confederacy instead. Lee surrendered to Ulysses S. Grant on April 9, 1865, ending the Civil War.

Abraham Lincoln (1809–1865). Sixteenth president of the United States, Lincoln led the nation through the Civil War. Known for his eloquent speeches, Lincoln is most famous for his Gettysburg Address and for successfully passing the Emancipation Proclamation that freed all slaves in the wake of the Civil War.

Marilyn Monroe (born Norma Jean Baker, 1926–1962). Actress legendary for her sex appeal, grace, and charisma. Monroe acted in twenty films and was married to baseball legend Joe Dimaggio and playwright Arthur Miller. She died from an overdose of sleeping pills.

Richard M. Nixon (1913–1994). Thirty-seventh president of the United States, Nixon was the first president to resign from office (to avoid impeachment). As president, Nixon ended the war with Vietnam and opened relations with China. His involvement in the Watergate scandal led to his political downfall.

Scarlett O'Hara. Strong-willed and sometimes ruthless character in Margaret Mitchell's Pulitzer Prize-winning novel, *Gone with the Wind.*

Rosa Parks (1913–). Civil rights activist whose 1955 refusal to give up her seat to a white passenger on a bus in Montgomery, Alabama sparked a citywide, 382-day boycott. The boycott led the Supreme Court to pronounce segregated seating unconstitutional.

Edgar Allan Poe (1809–1849). Poet, short-story writer, and literary critic, Poe is best known for his terrifying and bizarre tales. He disdained the didactic writing style of the day, embracing verse instead. His best known works are the poem "The Raven" and the short stories "The Murders in the Rue Morgue," "The Fall of the House of Usher," and "The Tell-Tale Heart."

Elvis Presley (1935–1977). Rock musician and cultural phenomenon, Presley was deeply influenced by gospel, country, and rhythm and blues. Controversial and banned in many areas for the outrageous gyrating of his hips, Presley became an internationally celebrated icon, still revered by countless fans as "the King."

Ronald Reagan (1911–). Fortieth president of the United States. An actor, Reagan appeared in over fifty films, many of them Westerns. A popular president, Reagan lowered inflation and kept down unemployment, but his tax cuts for the wealthy and increased military spending during the Cold War era raised the federal deficit to unprecedented highs.

Paul Revere (1734–1818). Patriot and Revolutionary War hero for his 1775 legendary horseback ride to warn Samuel Adams and John Hancock that the British were approaching. A leader of the Sons of Liberty, Revere participated in the Boston Tea Party and used his skills as a silversmith to engrave political cartoons and propaganda for the colonial cause.

Eleanor Roosevelt (1884–1962). Activist First Lady, humanitarian, and diplomat. Roosevelt used a newspaper column, radio show, travels, and press conferences to advocate in support of underprivileged and minority groups. As a member of the United Nations General Assembly, she helped draft the Universal Declaration of Human Rights in 1946.

Betsy Ross (1752–1836). Patriot and seamstress believed to have made the first American flag at George Washington's request in 1776.

Babe Ruth (born George Herman Ruth, 1895–1948). Baseball Hall-of-Famer, legendary for his home runs. Ruth set a record of sixty home runs in 1927 with the New York Yankees. A crowd pleaser, Ruth galvanized the sport, leading the Yankees to four championships and boasting a career 712 homeruns and a .342 lifetime batting average.

Homer Simpson. Father in the animated television hit comedy *The Simpsons*, created by Matt Groening. Best known for his much-emulated annoyed grunt, "D'oh!"

Sitting Bull (Tatanka Iyotake, 1831–1890). Sioux leader of the Hunkpapa tribe. He provided counsel and aid to his tribe during the battle of Little Bighorn in 1876, also known as Custer's Last Stand. Chief Sitting Bull urged the Sioux to resist giving up their lands. Seen as a threat to peace, Sitting Bull was arrested and ordered to a military compound. But he was killed en route for allegedly resisting arrest.

Gertrude Stein (1874–1946). Writer, whose original writing style is based on simplification, word repetition, and little punctuation: "Rose is a rose is a rose is a rose." A pioneer in "stream of consciousness" writing, she was an influence on the artistic vanguard of her time in Paris, including Ernest Hemingway, Sherwood Anderson, and Pablo Picasso.

Shirley Temple (Black) (1928–). Child film star whose career, begun at age three, included starring roles in twenty-five films. Temple retired from the movies in 1949 and began her career as a stateswoman, with stints at the U.S. State Department, as a U.S. representative to the United Nations, and as an ambassador to Ghana and then to Czechoslovakia.

Martha Washington (1731–1802). The very first First Lady and wife of George Washington. She traveled with George Washington during the Revolutionary War to mend clothes for soldiers and uplift Washington's morale at Valley Forge, Pennsylvania, and Morristown, New Jersey.

John Wayne (born Marion Michael Morrison, 1907–1979). Actor who starred as the tough hero in all but eleven of the 250 films he made—mostly Westerns and war action movies. Known as "Duke," Wayne's breakthrough movie was John Ford's *Stagecoach* in 1939.

Compiled by Leif Ottesen

My deepest thanks to the wonderful people whose words and images grace these pages.
Your stories, expressions, and advice will be with me always.
And the kindness and generosity you showed a stranger will forever color the way I see the world.

**Earnest thanks to the honorary Great Americans staff, my confidantes, editors,
transcribers, and traveling companions: erin, karen, leif, nancy, nandu, nicko, tim, yansi,
beth, cyn, candice, dad, flo, grandma, jean & ken, suraiya,**

. . . and most of all, mom, without whom this wouldn't have happened.

Thanks also to all the folks who gave me shelter and company on the road, and other vital assistance:
alan, alicia, alison, amy, andy, annette, babe, ben, betty jean, bob, caroline, dad, darla & john, dave, eldon & katie,
greg, gualberto, the horowitzes, jessie, jon, john henry, jonah, koren, the lehmanns, lisa, lucy, marilyn & barb,
mara, mark, marta, morgan, nish, ray, shauna, the sickles, steve, the tallies, and tom.

Finally, thanks to elizabeth for believing in this book and for finding its perfect home in the hands of
colin, karen, alan, amanda, greg, elizabeth @ hello, and the rest of the bloomsbury crew.

If work is love made manifest, here's a whole lot of love.